# Sleeping With My Inner Me

Dr. Glenda Brown-Akiens, Ph.D.

Unless otherwise indicated, all Scripture quotations are taken from the King James Version of the *Bible*.
Copyright 2010 by Glenda Brown-Akiens
ISBN 1492349399
ISBN-13 978-1492349396
All rights reserved. No part of this book may be reproduced or transmitted in any form or by any means without written permission from the author.
Printed in the United States of America.
Cover design by Christina Jones, Fly Major Graphics
 www.flickr.com/fmgraphic
Image courtesy of Keenen Browne / www.livemilliyonic.com

# Contents

| | |
|---|---|
| i. | Dedication |
| ii. | Abstract |
| iii. | Introduction |
| I. | Spirit, Body And Soul |
| II. | Where Did Man Sin Originate From |
| III. | Renewing Your Mind |
| IV. | Forgetting The Things Behind |
| V. | Sleeping with My Inner Me |
| VI. | What Is Shame |
| VII. | Fear |
| VIII. | Hurt People, Hurt People |
| IX. | Wounded Heart |
| X. | Combination Code |
| XI. | Deliverance |
| XII. | Relationship |
| XIII. | Life Healing Changes |
| XIV. | Conquering Your Flesh |

## DEDICATION

This book is dedicated to my loving husband Dr. Latera Akiens and my daughters Yolanda, Danielle, Sherry, and Akiya. With gratitude to my Pastors Ralph and Janet White and those that helped me with my brokenness. Especially to Dr.__ that God sent along to help reveal His truth unto me and my husband. I stated to you the first time that I met you that God sent you just for me.

# Abstract

The goal of this book is to help the Body of Christ reach their full potential through healing and deliverance. The word states that no man will be able to stand before the Father and say that they had not heard the truth once. All the steps that we are taking by speaking words of truth and striving to manifest the light that we have already received, are carrying us on swiftly to the time when we shall consciously have the perfect mind of Christ, with all the love and beauty and health and power which that implies.

There is not a single key that unlocks the mystery of one's life issues, but a combination code that uncovers the secret to opening each person's door of bondage that allows them to be set free. Each part of the combination has to be identified and dealt with through acknowledging and accepting the truth about one's self. Failure to acknowledge and accept the truth on any level prohibits a complete and successful breakthrough. These symptoms are indications of conflicts between your inner self and outer self. This book helps you to find the keys that unlock the mystery of your life issues and then open that door that holds you in bondage.

The Word states that for everything there is a time and a season and if you are reading this, it is not by accident. It means that God is trying to get your attention. There is a pulling and uneasiness in your spirit that you are not sure of, but you know there has to be more of God. God is requiring a full and complete change of each person. It is the understanding and acceptance of one's unique self through healing. *Sleeping with My Inner Me* prompts each individual to allow God to effect change in his or her life. Your deliverance is here! Surrender to the Lord Jesus Christ and His plan for your life.

Surrender is a willingness to let go of your ungodly ways and replace them with methods that are taught in the Holy Scriptures. This is a daily surrender. We are spiritual beings created by God with a precise order and balance of body, soul, and spirit. The spirit encompasses God's imprint upon each of our hearts and is the binding, blending, and balancing agent within our being.

It is a revelation about our consciousness, spirit, soul, and the body of God within us as omnipotent power, so that we can, by a word or a look, "accomplish that whereunto the word is sent." We want the manifestation of the Father in us so that we can know Him personally. We want to be conscious of *"God working in us to will and to do"* (Philippians 2:13) so that we may *"work out our salvation."* (Philippians 2:12) We have been learning how to do the outworking, but we have now come to a point where our spirit man is calling us to learn more of how to be conscious of the divine inner working and Gods truth.

What has you in bondage? Jesus said, *"The Spirit of the Lord is upon me, because he hath anointed me to preach the gospel to the poor; he hath sent me to heal the brokenhearted, to preach deliverance to the captives... to set at liberty them that are bruised (crushed)."* (Luke 4:18) By definition; deliverance is either the act of delivering someone or it is the state of being delivered. *"Now the Lord is that Spirit: and where the Spirit of the Lord is, there is liberty* (freedom)" (Luke 4:18).

  The Father knows your needs and He cares for you. Through this book, The Father desires for you to be free from the hurt that life brings upon you and delivered from whatever has you bound in shackles of despair. *"The Lord is nigh unto them that are of a broken heart; and saveth such as be of a contrite spirit".* (Psalms 34:18) Psalms 86:7 states, *"In the day of my trouble I will call upon thee: for thou wilt answer me."* The Lord will answer thee because *"The word of the Lord endureth for ever."* (1 Peter 1:25)

# Introduction

This book is based off of over nine years of my ministry. It is part of my own personal life as well as others because in order for something to be truth for you, you have to live it. Every part of this book has been battle ground tested to help you through the situations you go through in this journey called life.

*Sleeping With My Inner Me* was birthed to help the children of God to trust Him and lean not on their own understanding, but to have faith in the Word of God. It lets you know that healing is the children's bread. Everything we go through in life is not just for us, but just like Jesus, He went through all His sufferings on our behalf.

We all have past hurts and failures that we must learn to let go of. We must not allow these hurts and failures to have power over us, continuing to drag us down and stopping us "dead in our tracks" from moving forward, meeting and conquering new challenges. Allowing these hurts and failures to rule our lives keeps us in a depressed or in a "funky" mood.

There is no need to continue reliving the hurts and frustrations of your past over and over again. Heartaches may continue to weigh heavy on our spirits as we cling to the pain, bitterness and disappointment of past hurts and failures. Understand that you are not destined to a life of unending burden and conflict. You are destined to live a FULL and complete life - a life complete with what you REALLY want!

# Chapter One

## Spirit, Body and Soul

Anyone who loves God will discover sooner or later that the greatest hindrance he or she has is not others, but themselves. They will discover that their soul (outer man) is not in harmony with their spirit (inward man). Both tend to go in opposite directions from each other. They will also sense the inability of their outer man to submit to the inner control of their regenerated spirit, received through the new birth. Thus, they are rendered incapable of obeying God's highest commands. They will quickly detect that their greatest difficulty lies in them not letting go of the things in their past (soul/flesh), which hinders them from using their spirit.

Notice how the Bible separates man into two parts:

*"For I delight in the Law of God in my inmost self"* (Romans 7:22) Our inward man delights in the Law of God *"To be strengthened and reinforced with mighty power in the inner man by the Holy Spirit Himself indwelling your innermost being and personality."* (Ephesians 3:16) Paul also tells us, *"Though our outer man is (progressively) decaying and washing away, yet our inner self is being (progressively) renewed day after day."* (2 Corinthians 4:16) (Comparative Study Bible NIV/Amplified/KJV/ Updated NASB)

When God comes to indwell us by His Spirit with His life and power, He comes into our spirit. At the time when we are born again John 3:6 states what is born of (from) flesh is flesh (of the physical is physical); and what is born of the Spirit is spirit. This regenerated spirit located at the center of man's being is what we call the inward man (Spirit). Man is the last and highest manifestation of God as creative Divine Energy; the fullest and most complete expression of God. To him, therefore is given the dominion over all other manifestations. (Nee)

God is not only the Creative cause of every visible form of intelligence and life at its commencement, but each moment throughout its existence, He lives within every created thing as the life, the ever-renewing, recreating, up building cause of it. He never is and never can be for even a moment separated from His creation. How can even a sparrow fall to the ground without His knowledge! "And ye are of more value than many sparrows." (Matthew 10:31)

God Is. Man exists (from "ex-" meaning "out of" and "-sistence" meaning "to stand forth"). Man stands forth out of God. Man is a three-fold being made up of spirit, soul and body. Spirit - our innermost, real being; the deathless part of us; the I of us (which you and I know has never changed though our thoughts and circumstances may have change hundreds of times). This part of us is a standing forth of God into visibility. It is the Father in us. At this central part of his being every person can say, "*I and the Father are one,*" and speak only absolute truth.

*"That they all may be one; as thou, Father , art in Me, and I in thee, that they also may be one in us: that the world may believe that thou hast sent Me. And the glory*

*which Thou gavest Me I have given them; that they may be one, even as we are one. I in them, and thou in Me, that they may be made perfect in one; and that the world may know that thou hast sent Me, and hast loved them, as thou hast loved Me. Father; I will that they also, whom thou hast given Me, be with Me where I am; that they may behold My glory, which thou hast given Me: for thou lovedst Me before the foundation of the world* (Gospel of John 17:21-24). (Holy Bible King James Version)

    The spirit of man deals with the spiritual realm. It is that part of man in which the Holy Spirit dwells. The spiritual body or 'upper spirit' may be divided into three parts -- intuition, conscience and fellowship. The "conscience" is the door to your spirit. It is that which tells us right from wrong, by which we feel guilt. Sin makes the conscience dull and not sensitive to the Holy Spirit by searing it like a hot iron. The conscience is the door by which we open our spirit to the Holy Spirit.

    The "intuition" is the knower - that by which we perceive or sense things or circumstances. The "fellowship" area of our spirit is that which is made to have fellowship with God. It is impossible to fellowship without honesty and openness. Outside the sphere of this inward man indwelt by God is the soul. Its functions are our thoughts, emotions, mental realm and will. It is the seat of man's character (or what some call personality), his intellect, his emotions and his will. It is with the mind that a person understands.

    The outermost man is our physical body, characterized by its external instincts of sight, sound, smell, taste, and touch. The body is that part of man which deals with the physical realm. It is dominated by the five senses and is the vehicle by which we communicate to the outside world. It's quite evident that men are generally more conscious of the physical body and the soul, but they hardly recognize or understand their inner man, their spirit.

We must know that he who can work for or truly walk with God is the one whose spirit can be released. The basic difficulty of a servant of God lies in the failure of his spirit to break through his soul. Therefore, we must recognize before God that the first difficulty to our work is not in others, but in ourselves. Our spirit seems to be wrapped in a covering which cannot easily break forth. If we have never learned how to release our spirit by breaking through the soul, we are not able to serve or truly live the life God created for us.

Whether our lives are fruitful or not depends upon whether our flesh has been broken by the Lord so the Spirit can pass through this brokenness and come forth. The Lord wants to break our flesh in order for the Spirit to have a way out. When the Spirit is released, both unbelievers and other believers will be blessed.

The Lord tells us in John 12 *"Except the grain of wheat falling into the ground die, it abides alone; but if it die, it bears much fruit."* (vs. 24) What do you have that needs to die? Bitterness, self righteousness, depression, hopelessness, arrogance, haughtiness, pride, self, religion, gossip, unforgiveness, control, manipulation, or tradition?

Life is within the grain of wheat. But there is a shell, a very hard shell on the outside. As long as the shell is not split open the wheat cannot sprout and grow. "Except *the grain of wheat falling into the ground die...*" (John 12:24) What is this death? It is the cracking open of the shell through temperature and humidity working together in the soil.

Scripture continues by saying, *"He that loves his life shall lose it, and he that hates his life in this world shall keep it to life eternal"* (John 12:25). The Lord is showing us that our outer shell is our life identified as our soul life, while the life within is the eternal life which He has given to us. To allow the inner life to come forth, it is imperative that the outward life be replaced. Should the outward man (soul) remain unbroken, the inward (spirit) would never be able to come forth.

The question is not how thus to obtain life, but rather how to allow this life to come forth. When we say "we need the Lord to break us," this is not merely a style of speaking, nor is it only a doctrine. It is most vital that the Lord breaks us. It is not that the Lord's life cannot cover the earth, but rather we imprison His life. It is not that the Lord cannot bless the church, but that the Lord's life is so confined within us, nothing is flowing forth. If the soul (outward man) remains unbroken, we can never be a blessing to His church. And we cannot expect the Lord to bless the Word of God through us!

Those who come to God from a life of sin are filled with brokenness, emotional scars, hurts and rejection. They are bound and imprisoned to many habits and thought patterns. Many are still full of anxiety, worry and depression. They are benumbed, badly crushed and mentally confused. When we come to God, our sin of rejecting Him is forgiven (when we repent). We are born again; we receive a new life and a new heart and are taken into His Kingdom. However, there are many areas in our life that have been destroyed by sin. These areas are in need of restoration and transformation by the Holy Spirit.

Have you ever had this experience: someone is trying to tell you something important when suddenly a great heaviness and sleepiness comes over you? Have you ever had someone trying to tell you something important and it's as though this huge wall suddenly appears between yourself and the person talking to you and all you want to do is change the subject of the conversation? Have you ever been thinking about something and another thought come in?

If you have had this experience in which 'something' invisible tries to forcefully stop you from hearing something important that someone is trying to tell you, then something is trying to block you. I was taught to pay attention to my thoughts and that if I am thinking about something and my mind wanders to something else, that's just how easy our adversary can change our thoughts.

The idea that there is something nasty inside of us when we believe we are basically good people is, of course, bound to be upsetting. Most people will simply deny it. Some just don't want to know. They will find explanations for their behavior which minimize their need to exercise responsibility for what is actually a very common phenomenon. However, just as there are common colds and cancer in the world of diseases, so there are different kinds of problems in people. As I am sure you will agree physical health is important. So also is spiritual health.

"*Where do wars and fights come from among you? Do they not come from your desires for pleasure that war in your members? You lust and do not have. You murder and covet and cannot obtain. You fight and war. Yet you do not have because you do not ask. You ask and do not receive, because you ask amiss, that you may spend it on your pleasures. Adulterers and adulteresses! Do you not know that friendship with the world is enmity with God? Whoever therefore wants to be a friend of the world makes himself an enemy of God. Or do you think that the Scripture says in vain, "The Spirit who dwells in us yearns jealously*"? But He gives more grace. Therefore He says: "*God resists the proud, but gives grace to the humble.*"
  *"Therefore submit to God. Resist the devil and he will flee from you. Draw near to God and He will draw near to you. Cleanse your hands, you sinners; and purify your hearts, you double-minded. Lament and mourn and weep! Let your laughter be turned to mourning and your joy to gloom. Humble yourselves in the sight of the Lord, and He will lift you up*" (James 4:1-10). (Comparative Study Bible NIV/Amplified/KJV/ Updated NASB)

Now this passage may, at first glance, sound as though it's coming from a killjoy. You might be tempted to think to yourself, "Oh, this is just so *typical* of the way the Church destroys all joy. Just listen to it! We're told to mourn and be gloomy!" Well, my friend, there are times to mourn - when a loved one passes away, for instance. That's natural.

The Book of Ecclesiastes says there are times when certain emotions within us need to be released. There are times to be sad and they are natural and healthy. Those who refuse to mourn are, in fact, bottling healing feelings away inside themselves.

As stated in Breaking Free "Real freedom requires real work. A key part of the work involves God's Word. We hide God's Word in our hearts so that we might not sin against Him. (Psalms 119:11; Isaiah 61:1-4; 43:10; 43:6-7; 55:2; 26:3; and 43:2-3) God wants to do in your life what your mind has never conceived. (Moore)

Dr. Betty Price stated from her series Faith to walk in the Spirit that as man is made up of the three parts we must receive the infilling of the Holy Spirit *"It is the spirit that quickeneth; the flesh profiteth nothing: the words that I speak unto you, they are spirit, and they are life"* (John 6:63). (Hebrew-Greek Key Word Study Bible) And as in Acts 1:8 *"But ye shall receive power, after that the Holy Ghost is come upon you: and ye shall be witnessed unto me both in Jerusalem, and in all Judea, and in Samaria, and unto the uttermost part of the earth"* She stated that the word says you cannot really be a witness for God until you are filled with the Holy Spirit.

Then in Galatians 5:16–18, *"This I say then, Walk in the Spirit, and ye shall not fulfill the lust of the flesh. For the Flesh lusteth against the Spirit, and the Spirit against the flesh: and these are contrary the one to the other: so that ye cannot do the things that ye would. But if ye be led of the Spirit, ye are not under the law"*. (Price and Price)

## Chapter 2

## Where Did Man's Sin Originate From

Because of the sin of Adam, mankind fell from the glory and consciousness of God. Death entered the world through the fall of man. This refers to spiritual death which separated man from God. Through sin, spiritual death was bought into existence and has remained ever since then. Death always comes through sin. Note that Romans 5:12 tells us about this matter: *"Sin came into the world through one man."* Adam sinned and introduced sin into the world. Romans then says that *"death* (came into the world) *through sin."* Death is sin's unchanging result. Sin had to be judged **before there could be a rescue by the salvation of the Lord Jesus** (as a perfect human being). (Holy Bible King James Version)

It is man's triune nature which sins; therefore, it is man who must die. Only humanity can atone for humanity. Because sin is in his humanity, man's own death cannot atone for his sin. The Lord Jesus came and took human nature upon Himself in order that He might be judged instead of humanity. Untainted by sin, His holy human nature could therefore, through death, atone for sinful humanity. He died a substitute, suffered all penalty of sin, and offered His life as ransom for many.

When the Word became flesh, He included all flesh in Himself. As the action of one man, Adam represents the action of all mankind. Therefore, the work of one man, Christ, represents the work of all.

Why is it that the sin of Adam is judged to be sin of all men both present and past? Adam is humanity's head from whom all other men have come into the world. Similarly, the obedience of one man, Christ, becomes the righteousness of many. In both the present and past, Christ constitutes the head of a new mankind entered by a new birth.

Hebrews 7 illustrates this point. To prove that the priesthood of Melchizedek is greater than the priesthood of Levi, the writer reminds his readers that Abraham once offered a tithe to Melchizedek and received from him blessing. Therefore, Abraham's tithe offering and blessing was Levi's; how so? "He (Levi) was still in the loins of his ancestor (Abraham) when Melchizedek met him!" We know that Abraham begot Isaac, Isaac begot Jacob, and Jacob begot Levi. Levi was Abraham's great grandson. When Abraham offered the tithe and received a blessing, Levi was not born. At the time, neither were his father and grandfather. However, the Bible considers Abraham's tithe and blessing as Levi's. Insomuch as Abraham is lesser than Melchizedek, Levi too is of less account than Melchizedek.

This incident can help us to understand why Adam's sin is construed to be the sin of all men and why the judgment upon Christ is counted as judgment for all. It is simply because at the time Adam sinned, all men were presently in his loins. Likewise, when Christ was judged, all who would be regenerated were present in Christ. His judgment is hence taken as their judgment, and all who believed in Christ shall no longer be judged. Since humanity must be judged, the Son of God, even the man Jesus Christ, suffered in His Spirit, soul, and body on the cross for the sins of the world.

Let us first consider His physical sufferings. Man sins through His body, and there enjoys the temporary pleasure of sin. The body must then accordingly be the recipient of punishment. Who can fathom the physical sufferings of the Lord Jesus on the cross? Are not Christ's suffering in the body clearly foretold in the Messianic writings? *"...they have pierced my hands and feet."* (Psalm 22:16) The prophet Zechariah called attention to *"Him whom they have pierced."* (12.10) His hands, feet, brow, side, and heart were all pierced by men for sinful humanity. Many were His wounds and high ran His fever for the weight of His whole body hung unsupported on the cross. His blood could not circulate freely and He was extremely thirsty. Therefore, He cried out; *"My tongue cleaves to my jaws" –"for my thirst they gave me vinegar to drink."* (Ps 22:15, 69:21)

The hands must be nailed, for they love to sin. The mouth must suffer, for it loves to sin. The feet must be pierced, for they love to sin. The brow must be crowned with a thorny crown, for it too loves to sin. All that the human body needed to suffer was executed upon His body. Nonetheless, He suffered physically even to death. It was within His power to escape these sufferings. However, He willingly offered His body to endure immeasurable trails and pains, never for a moment shrinking back until He knew that *"all was now finished."* (John 19:28) Only at that moment did He dismiss His

Spirit. (Comparative Study Bible NIV/ Amplified /KJV/ Updated NASB)

Not only had His body suffered, but His soul as well. The soul is the organ of self-consciousness. Before being crucified, Christ was administered wine mingled with myrrh as a sedative to alleviate pain, but He refused it as He was not willing to lose His consciousness. Human souls have fully enjoyed the pleasure of sins. Therefore, in His soul, Jesus would endure the pain of sins. He would rather drink the cup given to Him by God than the cup which numbed consciousness.

The Bible records that the soldiers took the garments of the Lord Jesus. (John 19:23) He was nearly naked when crucified; making this is one of the shames of the cross. Sin takes our radiant garment away and renders us naked. Our Lord was stripped bare before Pilate and again on Calvary. How would His holy soul react to such abuse? Would it not insult the holiness of His character and cover Him with shamefulness? Who can enter into His feelings during that tragic moment? Because every man had enjoyed the apparent glory of sin, the Savior must endure the real shame of sin. Truly *"thou (God) hast covered Him with shame...with which thy enemies taunt, O Lord, with which they mock the footsteps of thy anointed"; He nonetheless "endured the cross, despising the shame."* (Psalm 89:45, 51 Comparative Study Bible NIV /Amplified /KJV / Updated NASB)

No one can ever ascertain how fully the soul of the Savior suffered on the cross. We often contemplate His physical suffering, but overlook the feeling of His soul. A week before the Passover, He was heard to have mentioned, *"Now is my soul trouble."* (John 12:27) This point to the cross! While in the Garden of Gethsemane, Jesus was again heard to say *"My soul is very sorrowful, even to death."* (Matthew 26:38) Were it not for these words, we would hardly think His soul had suffered.

Isaiah 53 mentions thrice how His soul was made an offering for sins, travailed, and poured out to death. (vv 10-12) Because Jesus bore the curse and shame of the cross, whoever believes in Him and walk after Him shall no more be cursed and put to shame. (Comparative Study Bible NIV /Amplified /KJV/ Updated NASB)

His spirit too suffered immensely. The spirit is the part of man which equips him to commune with God. The Son of God was holy, blameless, unstained, and separated from sinners. His Spirit was united with the Holy Spirit in perfect oneness; and because of that, never did there exist a moment of disturbance or doubt because He always had God's presence with Him. *"It is not I alone"*, declared Jesus, *"But I and Father who sent Me... And He who sent Me is with Me."* (John 8:16, 29) For this reason, He could pray. *"Father, I thank thee that thou hast heard Me. I knew that thou hearest me always."* (John 11:41-42) Nevertheless, while He hung on the cross---and if there ever were a day when the Son of God desperately needed the presence of God it must have been that day---He cried out *"My God, My God, why hast thou forsaken Me?"* (Matthew 27:46 Holy Bible King James Version)

Because His Spirit was split asunder from God, He intensely felt the loneliness, desertion, and separation. The Son was still yielding and obeying the will of the Father, God. Still, the Son was forsaken; not for His own sake, but for the sake of others. (His separation brought reconciliation for us to the Father).

Sin affects most deeply the spirit. Consequently, as holy as the Son of God was, He still had to be wrenched away from the Father because He bore the sin of others. It is true that in the countless days of eternity past, *"I and the Father are one."* (John 10:30) Even during His days of earthly sojourn this remained true; for His humanity could not be a cause of separation from God. Sin alone could separate, even though that sin was the sin of others. Jesus suffered this spiritual separation for us in order that our spirit could return to God. (Holy Bible King James Version) He was deprived of the Holy Spirit in His Spirit (Eph 3:16) because His Spirit was torn away from the Spirit of God. Therefore, He signed *"I am poured out like water, and all my bones are out of joint; my heart is like wax, it is melted within my breast; My strength is dried up like a potsherd, and my tongue cleaves to my jaws; thou dost lay me in the dust of death."* (Psalm 22:14-15 Holy Bible King James Version)

On the one side the Holy Spirit of God deserted Him, and on the other the evil spirit of Satan mocked Him. It seems apparent that Psalm 22:11 refers to this phase; *"Be not far from me...for trouble is near; for there none to help. Many bulls encamps me, strong bulls of Bashan have beset me around."* (Holy Bible King James Version) His spirit endured God's desertion on one side and resisted the evil spirit's derision on the other. Man's human spirit has so separated itself from God, exalted itself, and followed the evil spirit that man's spirit must be totally broken in order that it may no longer resist God and remain allied with the enemy.

The Lord Jesus became sin for us on the cross. His inner holy humanity was completely smashed as God passed judgment upon unholy humanity. Forsaken by God, Christ thus suffered sin's most bitter pain and endured in darkness the punitive wrath of God on sin without the support of the love of God or the light of His countenance. To be forsaken by God is the consequence of sin. Our sinful humanity has now been judged completely because it was judged in the sinless humanity of the Lord Jesus. In Him, holy humanity has won its victory. Whatever judgment should come upon the body, soul, and spirit of sinners has been poured upon Him. He is our representative and by faith we are joined to Him. His death is reckoned as our death, and His judgment as our judgment. Our spirit, soul, and body have altogether been judged and penalized in Him. It would not be any different had we been punished in person. *"There is therefore now no condemnation for those who are in Christ Jesus."* (Romans 8:1 Comparative Study Bible NIV/Amplified/KJV/ Updated NASB)

This is what Jesus has accomplished for us and such is now our standing before God. *"For he who has died is freed from sin."* (Romans 6:7) **(Already been to the cross!)** Position we have already died in the Lord Jesus; it only awaits the Holy Spirit to translate this fact into our experience. (Comparative Study Bible NIV/Amplified/KJV/Updated NASB)

In 1 Peter 1:13-16, he writes to believers "*Therefore, prepare your minds for action, keep sober in spirit, fix your hope completely on the grace to be brought to you at the revelation of Jesus Christ. As obedient children, do not be conformed to the former lusts which were yours in your ignorance, but like the Holy One who called you, be holy yourselves also in all your behavior; because it is written, 'You shall be holy, for I am holy.'*" Peter is quoting from Leviticus 11:44 and Leviticus 19:2. (Comparative Study Bible NIV/Amplified/KJV/Updated NASB)

First, let's look at God's holiness. What does it mean that God is Holy? Passages like 1 Samuel 2:2 and Isaiah 6:3 are just two of many examples of passages about God's holiness. Another way to say it is 'absolute perfection'. God is unlike any other (see Hosea 11:9), and His holiness is the essence of that "otherness". His very being is completely absent of even a trace of sin. (James 1:13 and Hebrews 6:18) He is high above any other and no one can compare to Him. (Psalm 40:5) God's holiness pervades His entire being and shapes all of His attributes. His love is a holy love, His mercy is holy mercy, and even His anger and wrath are holy anger and holy wrath. These concepts are difficult for humans to grasp, just as God is difficult for us to understand in His entirety.

What does it mean for us to be holy? When God told Israel to be holy in Leviticus 11 and 19, He was instructing them to be distinct from the other nations by giving them specific regulations to govern their lives. Israel is God's chosen nation and God has set them apart from all other groups of people. They are His special people, and consequently they were given standards that God wanted them to live by so the world would know they belonged to Him. When Peter repeats the Lord's words in 1 Peter 1:16, he is talking specifically to believers. As believers, we need to be "set apart" from the world unto the Lord. We need to be living by God's standards, not the world's. God isn't calling us to be perfect, but to be distinct from the world. 1 Peter 2:9 describes believers as a "holy nation". It is a fact! We are separated from the world and need to live out that reality in our day-to-day lives. Peter tells us how to do this in 1 Peter 1:13-16.

    Paul writes in his first epistle (1 Thessalonians 3:13; 4:7; 5:24): *"he may establish your hearts unblameable in holiness...God hath not called us unto uncleanness, but unto holiness...Faithful is he that calleth you, who also will do it"*. Holiness only results from a right relationship with God. If we have not placed our faith in God's Son alone to save us from our sins, then our pursuit of holiness is in vain. So, we must first make sure we are born-again believers. (See John 3) If we truly are believers, then we recognize that our position in Christ automatically sets us apart from the world. (1 Peter 2:9)

We have a relationship with the living God! We must live a set-apart life on a day-to-day basis, not trying to "blend in" with the world, but instead live according to God's Word as we study the Bible and grow in it. This is utterly impossible unless we take time and allow the holiness of God to shine on us. How can any man on earth obtain intimate knowledge of another man of remarkable wisdom, if he does not associate with him and place himself under his influence? How can God himself sanctify us if we do not take time to be brought under the power of the glory of His holiness? Nowhere can we get to know the holiness of God, and come under its influence and power, except in the inner-chamber.

What is this holiness of God? It is the highest and most glorious and most all-embracing out of all of the attributes of God. Holiness is the most profound word in the Bible. It is a word that is at home in heaven. Both the Old and New Testaments tell us this. Isaiah heard the Seraph's with veiled faces cry out, *"Holy, Holy, Holy, is the Lord of hosts."* (6:3) John heard the four living creatures say, *"Holy, Holy, Holy, Lord God Almighty."* (Revelation 4:8) This is the highest expression of God's glory in heaven; by beings that live in His immediate presence and bow low before Him. (Comparative Study Bible NIV /Amplified /KJV/ Updated NASB)

Let thy holiness, O Lord, shine more and more into our hearts, that they may become holy. Let our hearts be deeply ashamed of our prayerlessness, through which we have made it impossible for God to impart His holiness to us. Let us beseech God fervently to forgive us this sin, allure us by his heavenly grace, and strengthen us to have fellowship with Him, the holy God.

In order to redeem fallen man for His purpose, God came in the Son through incarnation to be the Lamb of God. (John 1:1, 14, 29) As the spotless Lamb of God offered Himself to the Father as our substitute, Christ died on the cross and shed His blood to take away the sin of the world. (John 1:29) 1 Peter 1:18-20 reveals that Christ was foreordained or prepared before the foundation of the world by God to be the redeeming Lamb. This means that the death of Christ was not an afterthought, but rather an integral component of God's original design.

The death of Christ is the last act of His humiliation in which He underwent extreme, horrible, and most acute pain for the sins of men. It was an act of Christ and not a mere matter of enduring because He met and endured it purposefully. John 10:11 says, *"I Am the Good Shepherd. The Good Shepherd lays down His life for His sheep."* 10:18 says, *"No man takes it from Me, but I lay it down Myself."* The act arose out of obedience to His Father and love for us, not out of His own guilt or deserving. The act was voluntary and not compelled. It was designed to satisfy through victory and not to ruin through surrender. (Comparative Study Bible NIV/Amplified/KJV/ Updated NASB) It contained the greatest punishment because it equaled all the misery which the sins of men deserved. Therefore, there is an abundance of words and phrases describing this death in the Scriptures. It is not simply called a death, but a cutting off, a casting away, a treading under feet, a curse, and a heaping up of sorrows. (Isaiah 53; Psalm 22)

The act also contained the punishments in such a way that their continuance and ordination to the uttermost, along with other circumstances accompanying the punishments of the sins of the lost, were removed from his death. Acts 2:24 states that "it could not be that He would be retained by death." There was in Christ both worthiness and a power to overcome as it was the punishment imposed. As 1 Corinthians 15:54-57 states, death is swallowed up in victory. This death was the consummation of all humiliation. It was by far the greatest part of that humiliation. Christ's death itself is often spoken of in the Scriptures by a synecdoche of the member as the full satisfaction of His whole humiliation. The death of Christ was the same in kind and proportion as the death justly due for the sins of men. The object of this wrath was not Christ because it was connected only with that punishment which He underwent as our surety.

The consummation of His death in conscious realization was the curse whereby he endured the full consciousness of God's judgment of man's sins. He was made a curse for us. The hanging on the cross was not a cause of or reason for this curse, but only a sign and symbol of it.

The Bible reveals that God's purpose for man is eternal, predating the fall, and that Christ's redemption is one step – an essential step in its fulfillment. According to this purpose, God wants to be intimately united with man by entering into man as life. (Genesis 2:2-9, 16 -17) However, due to his fall, man lost his qualification to receive the righteous, holy, and glorious God. He therefore needed to be redeemed in order to become a suitable vessel for the life of God. This is similar to the need to cleanse a dirty cup before pouring a beverage into it. The Bible reveals that man, like the cup, is a vessel and container. (Roman 9:20-24) As a case in point, the Lord Jesus specifically designated Paul as a *"chosen treasure in earthen vessels."* (2 Corinthians 4:7) This referred to Christ of glory (the treasure) within the believers (the earthen vessels). Vessels have a function unlike that of instruments or tools as they are meant to be filled. However, unless fallen man is washed through redemption, God cannot enter into him. Christ's redemption of man is for God's life-impartation into man. (Comparative Study Bible NIV/Amplified/KJV/ Updated NASB)

In his original, sinless state in the Garden of Eden, man was entitled to eat of the tree of life. However, after his fall in chapter three of Genesis, man forfeited this privilege. God therefore stationed cherubim with a flaming sword in front of the tree of life to guard it from sinful man. The tree of life represents God as the source of the divine life to man. The cherubim with the flaming sword guarding the tree of life represent the requirements of God's righteousness (sword), holiness (flame), and glory (cherubim). Accordingly, Paul pointed out that *"there is none righteous, not even one...for all have sinned and fallen short of the glory of God."* (Romans 3:10, 23) Nevertheless, through His death on the cross, Christ fully satisfied the requirements of God's righteousness, holiness, and glory that man may once again receive the life of God. Hence, when Christ came, He declared, "*I have come that they (redeemed humanity) may have life and may have it abundantly.*" (John 10:10b) By this statement, Christ indicated that through His death, He will restore to man the riches of the tree of life. (Comparative Study Bible NIV /Amplified /KJV/ Updated NASB)

According to Colossians 3:5, Christ is the believers' life. Christ came into the believers to be their life inwardly that He might begin to dwell within them, and gradually bring them into a complete union with God in Christ. The Lord Jesus prophesied this mutual indwelling to be accomplished on the day of His Resurrection. "*In that day you shall know that I Am in the Father and you in Me and I in you.*" (John 14:20) Thus the goal of Christ's redemption is not merely to save fallen sinners from hell or perdition, but through the forgiveness of sin, the impartation of life, and Christ's indwelling, bring them into union with the Triune God. Following redemption, believers are regenerated with the divine life (1 Peter 1:3) that they may eventually be transformed by life (2 Corinthians 3:18), glorified by life, (Philippians 3:21) and ultimately, be built up in divine life into the Body of Christ. (Ephesians 4:16) This comprehensive lifelong process cannot begin without the initial step of the redemption of Christ. (Comparative Study Bible NIV/Amplified/KJV/ Updated NASB)

The resurrection of Jesus Christ is the very heart of the Kingdom of God. In 1 Corinthians 15,

St. Paul reasoned, *"If Christ has not been raised, our preaching is useless and so is your faith. We are then found to be false witnesses about God, for we have testified about God that He raised Christ from the dead."* In that same chapter he says, "If Christ has not been raised, your faith is futile; you are still in your sins. Then those also who have fallen sleep in Christ are lost. If only for this life we have hope in Christ, we are to be pitied more than all men." Conversely, Paul triumphantly declares, *"But Christ has indeed been raised from the dead, the firstfruits of those who have fallen asleep."* (1 Cor. 15:14-20) (Comparative Study Bible NIV /Amplified /KJV/ Updated NASB)

  Jesus Christ came into this world to die as our substitute for our sins. The sinless Son of God came to give his life as a ransom for many. (Matt. 20:28) Jesus was crucified! We know He died because one of the Roman soldiers pierced Jesus' side with a spear to ensure his death. Some of his disciples then went on to bury his body in a new tomb. (John 19:30-42)

  While Jesus was alive, He had predicted that He would rise from the dead. He challenged His enemies to *"Destroy this temple, and I will raise it again in three days."* He was speaking about His body. (John 2:19-22) Jesus also told His disciples many times that He would be killed by the leaders in Jerusalem, but be raised to life on the third day. The leaders who killed Jesus were aware of this prediction that He would rise from the dead. Although they did not believe it, they wanted to ensure that it would not happen. Accordingly, they set a guard around the tomb. In Matthew 27:62-66, we read, "*The next day, the chief priests and the Pharisees went to Pilate, 'Sir,' they said, 'we remember that while He was still alive, that deceiver said, "After three days I will rise again."* In other words, give the order for the tomb to be made secure. Otherwise, His disciples may come to steal the body and tell the people that He has been raised from the dead. This last deception will be worse than the first. 'Take a guard', Pilate answered. 'Go; make the tomb as secure as you know how.' So they went and made the tomb secure by putting a seal on the stone and posting the guard. (Comparative Study Bible NIV/Amplified/KJV/ Updated NASB)

    Did the strategy of the chief priests and Pharisees succeed? No! Despite their efforts, Jesus rose from the dead. Remember how Jesus had said to Martha, "I Am the Resurrection and the Life"? During his ministry on earth, Jesus brought a number of people to life from the dead, including Martha's brother Lazarus, who had been dead for four days. (John 11) However, the resurrection of Jesus Christ was different. It was not just **resuscitation**, as was the case with Lazarus, who later died again. On the third day Jesus was raised from the dead with a transformed body that was clothed with immortality and glory. His resurrection body could appear and disappear, go through material objects, and ascend to and descend from heaven.

    In the resurrection of Jesus Christ, we see the clear demonstration of the power of the true God. Ephesians 1:19-21 tells us that it is the power of our heavenly Father that raised Jesus Christ from the dead. The resurrection proves that Jesus Christ is God. That is exactly what God the Father wanted to communicate to us, as we read in Romans 1:4. The resurrection of Jesus Christ demonstrates the truth that He is who He said He was. The resurrection of Jesus Christ demonstrates to us that all the teachings of Jesus Christ are true. Everything Jesus taught was true, along with His great promise in John 6:40 that *"Everyone who looks to the Son and believes in him shall have eternal life, and I will raise him up on the last day."* Jesus' teachings concerning His person, His work, heaven, hell, and the future judgment are all true. The resurrection of Jesus Christ secured our justification. *"Christ died for our sins and he was raised for our justification,"* says Paul in Romans 4:25. (Comparative Study Bible NIV/Amplified/KJV/ Updated NASB)

The resurrection of Jesus Christ demonstrates that Jesus Christ is going to be the appointed judge of all the wicked people in the world. In Acts 17:31, Paul told the Athenians, "For He [God] has set a day when He will judge the world with justice by the man He has appointed. He has given proof of this to all men by raising Him from the dead." We see the same idea in John 5:22 where Jesus said, *"Moreover, the Father judges no one, but has entrusted all judgment to the Son."* In verses 27-29 he continued, *"And He has given him authority to judge, because He is the Son of Man."* (Comparative Study Bible NIV/Amplified/KJV/ Updated NASB)

The resurrection is the triumphant and glorious victory for every believer. Jesus Christ died, was buried, and rose the third day according to the

Scripture. He is coming again! The dead in Christ will be raised up, and those who remain and are alive at His coming will be changed and receive new, glorified bodies. (1 Thessalonians 4:13-18)

"*Wherefore God also hath highly exalted him, and given him a name which is above every name: That at the name of Jesus every knee should bow, of things in heaven, and things in earth, and things under the earth; And that every tongue should confess that Jesus Christ is Lord, to the glory of God the Father.*" (Philippians 2:9-11)

"*For God sent not His Son into the world to condemn the world, but that the world through Him might be saved. He that believeth on Him is not condemned; but He that believeth not is condemned already, because he hath not believed in the name of the only begotten Son of God.*" (John 3:17-18) (Comparative Study Bible NIV/Amplified/KJV/ Updated NASB)

The problem is that "all have sinned, and come short of the glory of God." (Romans 3:23) Man, in his lost, sinful, and condemned state failed to glorify God. Until a person becomes personally and exceedingly sinful in his own eyes, he will never see his need for repentance. Ephesians.2:1 says that man is spiritually dead. Romans 3:10 and Isaiah 64:6 tell us no one is righteous before a holy God. Romans 3:19 says that all stand guilty and condemned before God. Ephesians 4:18 declares all sinners are separated from God whose hearts and minds are blinded so that they cannot understand God or the things of God.

The reason Jesus came to this earth was to call sinners to repentance. "*I am not come to call the righteous, but sinners to repentance.*" (Matthew 9:13) Those who did not see themselves as sinners, who were deserving of God's wrath, were not candidates for God's salvation. The sinner must reject his own righteousness, because Jesus did not come to call the righteous, not even the self-righteous. The only way a sinner will come to reject his own righteousness is by coming face to face with his own wickedness. You can take it from the lips of Jesus Himself as a settled issue that He will not call the righteous. Only those to whom it is revealed (by God's Spirit) that they are lost, depraved, ungodly sinners will respond to the calling of the Savior in salvation. (Holy Bible King James Version)

Jesus soundly declared the message in His day, "*repent ye, and believe the gospel.*" Repentance and faith are inseparable and occur simultaneously in a sinner's heart. For that reason, you cannot have one without the other. The order as given in the Bible is repentance and faith. (Mark 1:15; Acts 20:21; 26:20; 2 Timothy 2:25; Hebrews 6:1) (Holy Bible King James Version)

**Repentance is turning from sin, and faith is turning to Christ.** Repentance comes about through the convicting power of the Spirit of God using the Word of God to cause a change of attitude, action, and affection.

Saving faith is trust in and reliance on the Lord Jesus Christ as one's personal Lord and Savior. Saving faith believes with your heart; it is coming to

Christ, receiving Christ, looking to Christ, and calling upon Christ to save your soul.

Yes, Jesus said you must repent and believe the gospel, because the gospel of Christ is the power of God unto salvation, to everyone that believes. (Romans 1:16) The gospel, the good news for every sinner, is that Christ died on the cross for our sins, as our Substitute, and shed His precious blood to wash away our sins. He arose from the dead on the third day in order that we might have the forgiveness of sins and have eternal life through Him. Salvation of one's soul is the most important thing in this whole world.

However, repentance without faith is nothing more than remorse or regret. Faith without repentance makes Christ nothing more than a fire escape. There must be a work of repentance and faith upon the sinner's heart before salvation can become a reality. Repentance is caused by the working of the Holy Spirit, who takes the Sword of the Spirit and slays the sinner's self-righteousness, self - goodness, self-decency, self-esteem, and causes him to cry out. *"God be merciful to me a sinner." (Luke 18:13) "What must I do to be saved?"* (Acts 16:30) (Holy Bible King James Version)

Faith in Christ means trusting Christ's death on the cross as sufficient payment for one's sins and living his life in accordance with this truth. Faith then is more than an intellectual agreement that Jesus really is the Messiah, but knowing that He is. It involves a daily commitment to and trust in the God of the universe, who revealed himself in the person of Christ. A true faith then will result in God's transforming power in our lives, which will change us from the inside out.

Faith also involves trusting God when you do not have strong intellectual reasons to do so because He is trustworthy. This may seem unwise; yet if most of us were honest, we would have to admit that many of our everyday decisions in life do involve a certain degree of faith. Whether it's in people, principles, or things, we can never prove in a court of Law these things as totally reliable. We truly cannot cross a street, drive a car, sit in a chair, or choose a spouse without some degree of faith or trust. In the same way, faith involves trusting God when we have incomplete understanding.

To the Body of Christ, **faith** is confidence and **assurance**, but it's not self-confidence or self-assurance. Its confidence in someone else who you know can do anything, but wants to do it with you. It's a confidence you can live by. Its confidence that even if this someone isn't 'on your side' of an issue or battle or dispute, this someone is '*by* your side' working to make good things come of your life. That someone is Christ, who is there in your faith, thanks to what the Spirit does in you.

Nevertheless, God has revealed to us enough of Himself and His faithfulness so we can trust Him even if we do not fully understand everything He says. As a result we can trust God for what we don't know because of what He has revealed to us that we do know. Emilie Cady quotes, "Faith is something you decide to do, not something you feel like doing. Believing the truth doesn't make it true. It's true; therefore, we believe it". (Cady)

*"For if we, being enemies, were reconciled to God through the death of His Son, much more, being reconciled, we shall be saved by His life."* (Romans 5:10) Man was created with three parts; the spirit, soul, and body. (1 Thessalonians 5:23) The fall damaged all three parts of man. Man's spirit became deadened (Ephesians 2:1), his soul, corrupted (Genesis 6:5), and his body, the flesh of sin and death (Genesis 6:3; Romans 6:6; 7:24). In such a pitiful and ruined condition, man is utterly helpless to save himself and devoid of any hope of expressing God. (Holy Bible King James Version)

However, when the kindness and the love to man of our Savior God appeared, not out of works in righteousness, which we did, but according to His mercy, He saved us. He saved us through the washing of regeneration and the renewing of the Holy Spirit, whom He poured out upon us richly through Jesus Christ our Savior. He did so in order that having been justified by His grace; we might become heirs according to the hope of eternal life. (Titus 3:4-7)

Through the processes of regeneration, transformation, and glorification, and by His life, God is able to save every part of our being—spirit, soul, and body. In each step of the process, God saves us by dispensing His rich life into us. What a wonderful Savior God is, and what a complete salvation He has for us!

The work of Jesus in the world is two-fold. It is a work accomplished *for us* and destined to effect *reconciliation* between God and man. It is a work accomplished *in us*, with the object of effecting our *sanctification*. By the one, a right relation is established between God and us. By the other, is the *fruit* of the re-established order. By the former, the condemned sinner is received into the state of grace. By the latter, the pardoned sinner is associated with the life of God. How many express themselves as if when forgiveness (with the peace which it procures) has been obtained, all is finished and the work of salvation complete? They seem to have no suspicion that salvation consists in the health of the soul, and that the health of the soul consists in holiness. Forgiveness is not the re-establishment of health. It is but the crisis of convalescence. If God thinks fit to declare the sinner righteous, it is in order that He may by that means restore him to holiness.

However, justification through Christ means that there's been a change in the way that God views mankind. A person is considered 'not guilty' even though the unchangeable Law condemns that individual as a transgressor. In Christ, provision has been made to change the individual; but, for justification to be effected, a change of lifestyle is not a condition. God has changed man so that He becomes acceptable to Him. This means that man is '*considered* not guilty'.

Man, left to himself and his own resources, could never have achieved 'right-standing' with God as he couldn't have achieved anything else that would have been beneficial in restoring a right relationship with Him. Man can get the 'not guilty' verdict solely because God has done something to rectify the condemnation that rested upon every individual. The initiative to restore mankind through the cross is never with man, but with God. Therefore, it is God who justifies.

Another word for regeneration is rebirth; from which we get the phrase "born again." To be born again is opposed to and distinguished from our first birth, when we were conceived in sin. The new birth is a spiritual, holy, and heavenly birth signified by a being made alive in a spiritual sense. Our first birth, on the other hand, was one of spiritual death because of inherited sin. Man in his natural state is dead in trespasses and sins until we are made alive (regenerated) by Christ when we place our faith in Him. (Ephesians 2:1) After regeneration, we begin to see, hear, and seek after divine things; along with living a life of faith and holiness. Now Christ is formed in the hearts. We are now partakers of the divine nature, having been made new creatures. God, not man, is the source of this. (Ephesians 2:1, 8) It is not by men's works, but by God's own good will and pleasure. His great love and free gift, rich grace, and abundant mercy are the cause of it. These attributes of God are displayed in the regeneration and conversion of sinners.

Regeneration is part of the "salvation package," along with sealing (Ephesians 1:14), adoption (Galatians 4:5), reconciliation (2 Corinthians 5:18-20), and many other salvation concepts. Being born again or born from above is parallel to regeneration. (John 3:6-7; Ephesians 2:1; 1 Peter 1:23; John 1:13; 1 John 3:9; 4:7; 5:1, 4, 18) Simply put, regeneration is God making a person spiritually alive, or a new creation, as a result of faith in Jesus Christ. The reason regeneration is necessary is that prior to salvation, we are not God's children (John 1:12-13); rather, you are children of wrath. (Ephesians 2:3; Romans 5:18-20) Before salvation, you are degenerate. After salvation you are regenerated. The result of regeneration is peace with God (Romans 5:1), new life (Titus 3:5; 2 Corinthians 5:17), and eternal sonship. (John 1:12-13; Galatians 3:26) This regeneration is eternal and begins the process of sanctification, wherein you become the people God intended for you to be. (Romans 8:28-30)

The Bible is clear that the only means of regeneration is by faith in the finished work of Christ on the cross. No amount of good works or keeping of the law can regenerate the heart which from birth is *"deceitful and wicked above all things"*. (Jeremiah 17:9) This concept of the new birth is unique to Christianity. (Holy Bible King James Version)

*"Now I say, as long as the heir is a child, he does not differ at all from a slave although he is owner of everything, but he is under guardians and managers until the date set by the father. So also we, while we were children, were held in bondage under the elemental things of the world. But when the fullness of the time came, God sent forth His Son, born of a woman, born under the Law, so that He might redeem those who were under the Law, that we might receive the adoption as sons. Because you are sons, God has sent forth the Spirit of His Son into our hearts, crying, "Abba! Father"! "Therefore you are no longer a slave, but a son; and if a son, then an heir through God." (Galatians 4:1-7*

Comparative Study Bible NIV /Amplified /KJV/ Updated NASB)

Through spiritual adoption, believers are made to be sons of God, heirs with Abraham, and partakers of the promises of the covenant God made with the patriarch. Since believers are adopted, they are no longer slaves but sons, and if sons, then heirs of God through Christ. (Galatians 4:7) As sons of God, believers enjoy full claim to the inheritance of the kingdom of God, and can *"stand fast therefore in the liberty where which Christ hath made us free, and be not be entangled again with a yoke of bondage"*. (Galatians 5:1; NKJV) However, in order to truly understand this new relationship between God and believers, we must first comprehend the biblical understanding of sonship. (Holy Bible King James Version)

In contrast to believers as sons of God, non-believers are called sons of disobedience. (Ephesians 2:2; 5:6) These sons of disobedience live in the lusts of the flesh, indulging the desires of the flesh and of the mind, and are by nature children of wrath. (Ephesians 2:3) They are even called sons of the devil. (John 8:44) The barrier to a Father-son relationship with God is gripped tightly in the depraved nature of man. This is true even for the heirs of Abraham – those chosen by God for salvation through election to be his adopted children. (Ephesians 1:4, 5) Elect believers are as assuredly as depraved and sons of hell on the road to eternal punishment as are the reprobates before they come to faith in Christ. Before hearing and accepting the gospel of Christ, the elect are equally slaves to sin and are in bondage to the elemental things of this world.

However, when the fullness of the time came, God sent forth His Son, born of a woman, born under the Law, so that He might redeem those who were under the Law; so that we might receive the adoption as sons. The initiative of adoption always begins with the prospective parent, and God was the first to act in order to call his elect to himself, in order to adopt them as his sons and heirs. Galatians 3:26-29 says,

For you are all sons of God through faith in Christ Jesus. All of you who were baptized into Christ have clothed yourselves with Christ. There is neither Jew nor Greek, there is neither slave nor free man, there is neither male nor female; for you are all one in Christ Jesus. If you belong to Christ, then you are Abraham's descendants and heirs according to promise.

Sanctification involves more than a mere moral reformation of character brought about by the power of the truth. It is the work of the Holy Spirit bringing the whole nature more and more under the influences of the new gracious principles implanted in the soul in regeneration. In other words, **sanctification is the carrying on to perfection as well as the work begun in regeneration. It extends to the whole man.** (Romans 6:13; 2 Corinthians 4:6; Colossians 3:10; 1 John 4:7; 1 Corinthians 6:19) **It is the special office of the Holy Spirit in the plan of redemption to carry on this work.** (1 Corinthians 6: 11; 2 Thessalonians 2:13) The separation of men from sin as well as the separation of them unto God is God's own work. It was God who in the Old Dispensation set apart the firstborn unto Himself, so it is God who in the New Dispensation sets apart the believer unto Himself and separates him from sin. (Self)

## Chapter 3

## Renewing Your Mind

Because of the fall of man not controlling his tongue when he bit off the forbidden fruit in the Garden of Eden, man lost his consciousness. Man at the beginning of time was tempted. He was enticed to commit an immoral act. Now because of man's tongue, fall, and loss of consciousness, the battle of the mind began. In our mind comes this battle into existence, and now our mind is always at war. We must really recognize the importance of our thought life and the impact that it has on our emotions, bodies, and life. One of the most important spiritual exercises that we can put into practice for improved life is to monitor our thought life and renew our thinking so that it is 'healthy' and spiritual.

We are reminded of the importance of dwelling on positive thoughts. Every word that we speak brings and cares life or death. We must learn to control the tongue so that we can conquer our mind. Apostle Paul writes, "When he wants to do right, something on the inside fights with him." He tells us that there are things we should think on. *"Finally, brethren, whatsoever things are true, whatsoever things are honest, whatsoever things are just, whatsoever things are pure, whatsoever things are lovely, whatsoever things are of good report; if there be any virtue, and if there be any praise, think on these things."* (Philippians 4:8) In other words, we can choose our thoughts. The Law of sin that wars in us attacks our minds. The Bible tells us out of Philippians that we don't have to sit there and let our thoughts build a nest; that we can choose what we think on. (Comparative Study Bible NIV/Amplified/KJV/ Updated NASB)

The Bible also tells us that as a man thinketh in his heart, so is he. (Proverbs 23:7) So it's really important what we think on. In Romans 12:1 - 2, the Bible says, *"I beseech you therefore, brethren, by the mercies of God, that ye present your bodies a living sacrifice, holy, acceptable unto God, which is your reasonable service. And be not conformed to this world: but be ye transformed by the renewing of your mind."* (Holy Bible King James Version) The Bible says we can be transformed by the renewing of our minds. We need to set a course and make a total commitment to the Lord Jesus Christ by being a living sacrifice. The problem with a living sacrifice is that sometimes it wants to crawl off the altar, so we have to make course corrections in our thoughts. We have to have a heart that says, "God, I want You and I want Your way." Not only do we need to make a total commitment, but part of having a victorious Kingdom life requires that we take the next step and be transformed by the renewing of our minds.

We must be aggressive about what we think or speak in terms of the world; if we don't want the world's results. As we read in Philippians 4:8, we can choose what to think on. Whatsoever is lovely, just, of good report, think on these things. In the Old Testament, they would take the Word of God and put it on their doorposts and on their garments. It was constantly in front of them. God instructed that they were to talk about the Word of God night and day;

that they might observe to do what it said. They were also to tell all these things to their children. It's very important what we think on. It's very important that we keep the Word of God in front of us all the time in order to really have a life of victory. Romans 8:6 says, *"To be carnally minded is death,"* but the next part of that verse says, *"To be spiritually minded is life and peace."* (Holy Bible King James Version) It is life and it is peace to think on the things of the Spirit of God.

The Bible says in Isaiah 26:3 that God will "keep him in perfect peace whose mind is stayed upon Him." There are times during the day that we all need to make course adjustments, just like it says in Romans 12. We need to say, "God, those are wrong thoughts. I need to turn around and renew my mind and start thinking about the things that are lovely, just, and of good report." If you've got a stronghold, if you're in bondage, if you find yourself thinking things that you shouldn't be thinking, you need to catch yourself immediately.

The Bible says, if we will draw near to God, He will draw near to us. If we resist the enemy, he will flee from us. There are times in my life when I've let things slip and let depression rise up. At those times, it's hard to pick up the Bible, sit down, take a passage, and say, "God, this is what you say about me. This is who You say that I am. You are my strength." Did you know that your victory is just that simple? You need to say, "I'm going to resist what I'm letting the enemy do to me right now. I'm going to sit down and open the Bible, and I'm not going to just read some words on these pages, but I'm going to connect with the God behind these words. I'm going to let my mind be stayed upon Him. Lord, this is what You say about me. You say that I'm forgiven. You say that I'm cleansed. You say that nothing can separate me from Your love. When you sit there and just think about all of the good things that God has done for you, in just a few moments, you're going to forget about those other things.

The Scripture is really telling us that we need to replace those thoughts with God's thoughts. When we see these things coming against us and we're thinking something we shouldn't think, we need to immediately call to mind our new identity. We need to immediately turn to the Lord, connect with Him. We need to not just connect with words on a page, but with the God behind those words. The Bible tells us in Romans 8:6 that as we do, we will see the transformation, as well as the life and peace God gives us when our minds are stayed upon Him and the things of the Spirit. Think on these things, my brethren. Walk this day in the liberty and freedom that Christ has purchased for us. As a man thinks in his heart, so is he. We'll begin to act on those things. We'll begin to play those things out in our lives and it will destroy our lives. You see, the real spiritual warfare for the believer is really not resisting or rebuking the devil all the time, although there are times that we need to do that. Spiritual warfare has to do with what we're thinking on and what we're dwelling on. (Shaw)

Unless we renew our minds, we are not going to enjoy our relationship or rights and privileges as sons and daughters of God. God said that we are justified, sanctified, and redeemed. God said that we are blessed with all spiritual blessings in the heavenlies; God said He shall supply all our needs according to His riches in glory in Christ Jesus; God said He wished that above all things we would prosper and be in health as our soul prospers. All of these tremendous truths of the Word will have no effect in our lives because we cannot apply them until we first renew our minds to what the Word declares. The statements are eternally true but will not become a reality to us until we renew our minds. God's holy word has the power to cleanse our mind of worldly contamination, filling us with the knowledge of God while prayer strengthens our spirit and increases our wisdom. The word of God is our sword and an essential part of our spiritual armor. The Lord was showing me that as I am consistently renewing my mind through prayer and meditation in His word daily that He pushes worldly influences out and renews my thinking, transforming me into the image of Christ.

Therefore, I should strive to renew my mind by faithful prayer and Bible study in order to be conformed to the image of Christ, which is the perfect will of God. The more I read the Bible and understand and believe the truths, the easier it will be to renew my mind and to think on spiritual and 'healthy' thoughts. Knowing God and His truths better is the first key in living an abundant life. (http://christianity.helium.com/topic/4033-bible-study)

## Chapter 4

## Forgetting the Things Behind

After you accept the Lord Jesus Christ as your Savior, the next step is to come into a full surrender of your entire life over to God the Father so that He can start to lead you onto the path and call that He has ordained for your life. Jesus must now become Lord over your life, not just your Savior. Making Jesus Lord over your life means that you will now turn the reigns of your life over to Him for Him to handle. It's no longer your will but His will. You are no longer your own. You now belong to God and Jesus and no one else! You are bought with a price and created for a purpose.

The first step one takes before moving forward in their walk and call with God is learning how to let the past go. *"Forgetting what is behind and straining toward what is ahead, I press on toward the goal to win the prize for which God has called me heavenward in Christ Jesus"* (Philippians 3:13b-14 Comparative Study Bible NIV /Amplified /KJV/ Updated NASB) Nothing is more vital to the Christian life than to walk daily after their spirit. It is this that maintains us in a constant spiritual state, delivers us from the power of flesh, and assists us to obey God's will. This will also shield us from the assaults of Satan.

Once becoming a Christian you are to make a decision to turn your will and life over to the care of God. God establishes your surrendered heart as the center from which your examination begins.

Committing yourselves to a life of abandonment to God, you are no longer operating from a self-centered position and "wallowing" is counter-productive to true recovery and sanctification. Which of us is exempt from this exhortation?

You can have the future you were predestined to have - *"God tells you to forget the former things in your life"* (Isaiah 43:18-19, Holy Bible KJV) It may be disconcerting and scary at times, but that's exactly what you have to do - put aside the past in order to enter into the future that God has planned for you. *"Before I formed you in the womb I knew (and) approved of you (as My chosen instrument), and before you were born I separated and set you apart, consecrating you (and) I appointed you as a prophet to the nations"* (Jeremiah 1:5). *"The word states "the steps of a good man are ordered by the Lord; and He delighteth in his ways"* (Psalm 37:23). (Comparative Study Bible NIV/Amplified/KJV/ Updated NASB)

Many Christians are not able to do even the most elementary work. Ordinarily, they should be enabled by the exercise of their spirit to know God's Word, to discern the spiritual condition of another, to send forth God's messages under the anointing, and to receive God's illumination. Yet, due to the distractions of not forgetting the things behind, their spirit does not seem to function properly. It is basically because unresolved issues have never been dealt with. As you shall see, only one kind of basic dealing can enable you to be useful before God and that is **brokenness - letting go of the things behind**

**you, letting go and letting God the Holy Spirit take control.**

The scriptures are replete with the call to live a reflective and introspective life as it relates to matters of your interior world. Lamentations 3:40 challenges us to *"...examine our ways and test them, and...return to the Lord".* The contemplative life of the poet, King David is the powerful model for this in the scriptures. *"Search me, O God, and know my heart, test me and know my anxious thoughts. See if there is any offensive way in me, and lead me in the way everlasting."* (Psalm 139:23-24 Comparative Study Bible NIV /Amplified /KJV / Updated NASB) One cannot surrender that which remains hidden and unknown.

Jesus said that He has come to set the captives free. One of the areas that you have to be set free from is wrong thinking that has arisen from the bad things that have occurred in your past. As you will see in the two verses listed below, Jesus and the Apostle Paul are telling you that you have to learn to let the past go. Jesus says that anyone who is trying to move forward in his walk for God, but keeps looking back, is not fit for the kingdom of God.

Paul says that the one thing he makes sure to do in his walk with God is to forget those things which are now behind him and press forward into those things which lie ahead of him. Once you put these two verses right next to one another, you get perfect revelation from the Lord on this issue.

You must know that he who can work for God is the one who's able to let God the Holy Spirit work a new thing in them. Then they can be released from the things of their past whether they be good or bad. The basic difficulty of the children of God lies in the failure of letting go of the past and to break through his outward man (soul/flesh). Therefore, you must recognize the difficulty is in you and not in others. It is as though your spirit is wrapped in a covering which cannot easily break forth. If you are focused on what's behind you'll never get what lies ahead. If you have never learned how to release the things from your past by letting The Holy Spirit break through the outward man (soul/flesh the hurt, pain, resentment, unforgiveness and bitterness), you are not able to serve. Nothing can so great hinder you than self. Whether your works are fruitful or not depends upon whether you can forget the things behind and press toward the prize of a high calling in Christ Jesus. Outward man (soul/flesh) has been broken by the Lord so that the inward man (spirit) can pass through this brokenness and come forth. The Lord wants to break you free from the things in your past.

      Whether or not you are able to accept it as the way of going on with God fully, the fact is that all of the soul's energies and abilities for knowing, understanding, sensing, and doing will come to an end. Subsequently you will stand bewildered, dazed, numb, and impotent. Only another constraint and only the divine energy will give you the strength to keep you going. In such times, you shall have to say to your souls: "*My soul, be thou silent unto God*" (Psalm 62:5) "*My soul, come thou with me to follow the Lord*". But what joy and strength there is when the soul has been constrained to yield to the spirit. Eventually, the higher wisdom and glory, derived from such suffering experience, will be recognized as its vindication. Then it is that praise and worship will break forth: "*My soul doth magnify the Lord, and my spirit hath rejoiced in God my Savior.*" (Luke 1:46 Comparative Study Bible NIV/Amplified/KJV/ Updated NASB)

Let's consider Saul (later, Paul) before he met the risen and gloried Jesus on the road to Damascus. He was no slouch among the Israelites of his day. By his own admission, he was the cream of the crop. Few could match his pedigree, his zeal to stand for what he knew as a Pharisee, or his righteousness in the Law. "*If anyone else has a mind to put confidence in the flesh, I far more: circumcised the eighth day, of the nation of Israel, of the tribe of Benjamin, a Hebrew of Hebrews; as to the Law, a Pharisee; as to zeal, a persecutor of the church; as to the righteousness which is in the Law, found blameless*". (Philippians 3:4-6 Comparative Study Bible NIV/Amplified/KJV/ Updated NASB)

But, when Jesus met him on that road to Damascus and blinded him with His glory, Saul's entire religious view and his confidence in the flesh were turned upside down. Paul started down a path that left his past on the dusty road to Damascus as he pressed on toward a new goal. His declaration was: **Forgetting what lies behind and reaching forward to what lies ahead.**

There are two ways to look back at the past. One is to consider all the good that one has done, and the other is to look at some offense or hurt that was never resolved or healed. Paul was in the first group. He had much to brag about and surely those of the circumcision would have reminded him of all his good. After all, as Saul, Paul had every reason to be proud of his flesh under Judaism. His confidence in the flesh was sevenfold. <u>First</u>, he was no proselyte to the commonwealth of Israel, for he was circumcised on the eighth day, as required. <u>Second</u> he was of the stock of Israel, a son of Abraham according to the blood line of Jacob. <u>Third</u>, he was of the tribe of Benjamin, one of the two tribes that held to the house of David, not one of the ten tribes that became apostate. <u>Fourth,</u> he was a Hebrew of Hebrews meaning that both his father and his mother were Hebrew; he was no mixed breed of Hebrew and gentile as so many were in his day.

Then, with regard to his conduct concerning Moses, he had three more confidences. <u>Fifth</u>, in relation to the Law, he was of the Pharisees who were the orthodox of Judaism unlike the Sadducees. <u>Sixth</u>, as to zeal, he was a persecutor of the church of Christ, which was a badge of honor for an orthodox Jew. <u>Seventh,</u> as to righteousness according to the Law, he proved blameless. Found blameless, as if blameless in the sight of God is not the intended meaning. Saul was blameless as viewed by the nation of Israel, for he was seen as one who had done all that was required and he had not transgressed the Law. In other words, when Saul turned from Moses to Christ, he had, so to speak, a clean bill of health under the old covenant.

Paul put it all behind him. He considered it all as loss for the sake of gaining Christ. He saw himself in a race and anything that weighed him down was thrown off so that he could finish his course and receive the prize that was set before him in the day of Christ. Paul's entire perspective changed dramatically after he met the risen and glorified Christ on the road to Damascus. When his blinded eyes were opened, he had a new goal set before him and to him. This goal was what mattered most. **But one thing I do!** What was that one thing? It was to forget all past that has great value according to the flesh. His confidence turned from the flesh and righteousness under the Law to the Person of Christ Jesus who became his righteousness by faith. Counting his past as rubbish and casting it aside, Paul set his sight on running the race in order to win the prize. In essence Paul got a new garment, a new mantle. The old garment and the old mantle were removed. Paul changed internally and externally, forgetting those things which were behind him.

Paul *"remember not the former things*; neither consider the things of old". He let God do a "new thing" in him at the time. "He did not know it", but God *"made a way in the wilderness and rivers in the desert"* for him. (Isaiah 43:18-19 Holy Bible KJV) We must be like Paul - willing to reach for the prize and forgetting those things behind and pressing toward the goal of Jesus. It's very important that we do not act like Lot's wife and look back when one should be looking and moving forward. Lot's wife did not trust what the angels of the Lord told them. She did not trust in God's Word that He would lead them. She trusted in herself.

Paul allowed the tearing down of things in his past. His incorrect thinking patterns or perceptions of Jesus had been burned into his way of thinking. If Paul had perceived that he himself was dirty and shameful full of failures, then he would not had been confident in his relationship with God.

Bottom line, you have to learn how to let your past go before you can start to proceed full steam ahead in your walk and call for the Lord. If you don't learn how to let the past go you will stay grounded and stuck right where you are, and you will never accomplish what God has for you to do in this life. You can choose to stay bound up in your past, continue to throw pity parties, and blame everyone and everything for your miseries. You can also choose to rise up and make a brand new fresh start with the Lord by choosing to fully surrender your entire life into His hands. Work with Him to get your past cleaned up so that you can fully start living in the present and walk into the call and destiny that He has already planned out for you; before you were even born into this world.

The choice to let the Holy Spirit help you to let go of your past so that you can start to fully live in your present is an individual choice for each believer. Not even God Himself will trample on your free will in this. All God can do is give you the knowledge, that this is what He wants from you. All of it is for your own good and then God will take you back in your past so that you can get all your loose ends tied up.

However, after that time is up, God will expect you to make a very important decision for your life. Will you now let your past go so that you can walk into the life and call that God now wants to give you? Or, will you choose to stay grounded, waiting in the misery of your past? Each Christian will have to make that choice. That is why the Bible says that you are transformed by the renewing of your mind. You have to learn how to develop right thinking in your thought process with how you think and how you view things. One of the first basic things you will need to learn and think right about is this principle of learning how to forget those things that are behind. (Bullock)

## Chapter 5

## Sleeping With My Inner Me

We all have past hurts and failures that we must learn to let go. We must not allow these hurts and failures to have power over us, or continue to drag us down and stop us "dead in our tracks" from moving forward to meet and conquer newer challenges. Allowing these hurts and failures to rule our lives keeps us in a depressed or "funky" mood. This affects our attitude, relationships, behavior on our jobs, and almost every area of our life. Who in their right mind wants to be around a crabby, pessimistic soul?

There is no need to continue reliving the hurts and frustrations of your past over and over again. Heartaches may continue to weigh heavy on our spirits as we cling to the pain, bitterness, and disappointment of past hurts and failures. Understand that you are not destined to a life of unending burden and conflict. You are destined to live a FULL and complete life. A life complete with what you REALLY want! Every time that you remember a past hurt, look at it square in the face and praise God for it. You "didn't" like it when it happened. It was a bad time in your life, but look at what the Lord is doing for you now. So praise the Lord and keep praising Him. Soon those past hurts won't hurt you anymore. They will just be a past memory.

Past hurts and failures can afflict the inner person, cause problems, and disrupt a person's life. If you recognize past hurts or emotional wounds interfering with your life, take hope. Jesus still heals, and His healing includes past hurts.

Inner healing is helping someone through the healing process. There is a need to talk about the hurts of the past, no matter how painful. Sometimes a person has never before done so. What we should be willing to embrace is the one where or "inner healing" really means the sanctification and transformation of the inner life through the cross and the resurrection life of Jesus Christ. People can be helped through prayer counseling where they are encouraged to respond to this self-humbling and facing of the truth. God will work by His Spirit and bring cleansing and a transformation in the life of the person receiving ministering. The more we learn to put off the old nature, the more the life of Jesus can shine through us. This is a big part of God's purpose for our lives.

Some people are very aware of a sense of being "wounded" by these experiences of the past. Other people are not actively aware that they were negatively affected or "wounded". In many cases, they may not even be aware that their environment or experiences were not "normal" because it is all they knew when they were young. Later in life, they did not desire to reexamine those memories. Even though there is a lack of awareness, their lives may still be hampered by certain characteristic problems such as self-esteem difficulties, feelings of guilt and shame, lack of emotional control (and/or being over-controlled), excessive or unexplained fears or sadness, compulsive behaviors, and difficulties with intimate relationships.

In Inner Healing of our past we work together with the Holy Spirit to understand our memories and the impact they have in our life. We especially work together to know how they connect to present-day emotions, behaviors, and relationships. As we go along our way, there is often a need to grieve the losses of the past - perhaps the loss of innocence, the loss of trust, the loss of a significant relationship, or the loss of a major part of one's childhood. Grieving involves facing those losses and includes a variety of emotions. Grieving is our way of preparing to let go, rather than covering up or avoiding and getting ready to move forward with our lives in a less encumbered way.

It is an inner healing of your past that involves letting God heal you of the guilt, shame, resentment, and/or whatever that's hindering you from going forth in the purpose and destiny God has created you for. This may involve a process of God revealing to you that you have unforgiveness in your heart for someone that you are not aware of. God states that *"the heart is deceitful above all things and desperately wicked who can know it?"* (Jeremiah 17:9) Psalm 139:23 states *"Search me, O God, and know my heart: try me, and know my thoughts."* Jesus stated in John 8:32, *"And ye shall know the truth, and the truth shall make you free."* He states in John 8:36 that *"If the Son therefore shall make you free, ye shall be free indeed."* The more our inner self is healed, the more the life of Jesus can shine through us. This is a big part of God's purpose for our lives. (Comparative Study Bible NIV/Amplified/KJV/ Updated NASB)

In other words, the foundation for our later life is laid in childhood. When a house needs fixing, major cracks and inadequacies in the foundation cannot be adequately compensated for in any other way but by giving attention directly to the foundation. I believe it is wise and most important to seek understanding and healing for our past as well as our present. Time alone does not and cannot heal those memories that are so painful that the person's mind cannot tolerate them. Our memory has the ability to block out of our mind things that we are not able to face. Our fears will not, and cannot allow us to lower our defense so that our buried memories can come out of hiding. This is true for individuals where there has been major dysfunction in their family of origin; but it is also helpful in the more minor problems that every one of us faced in our childhood years. For example, look at this young's man story. He never knew that he was in bondage or what was holding him in the funk that would come and go in his life.

**My name is Tawan and this is my story of Deliverance and Healing.** *All of my life I had been living a lifestyle that I did not belong in and did not deserve. I did not know this lifestyle was not for me until one day when I felt I truly heard from God. He told me that if I did not turn from this lifestyle, He would turn me over to a reprobate mind.*

*My life changed one day in November of 2008 when I talked with someone in my family and they told me about this man and woman of God from Tennessee. So, one night I called Glenda and Latera Akiens who had a Healing and Deliverance ministry. I called crying and asking for help. I needed healing and deliverance from the lifestyle of homosexuality. They told me their ministry was restoring God's people back to His truth.*

*I was first told that they did not judge me, that God was the only Judge and that they loved me and that God also loved me. I was led through a prayer of repentance for my lifestyle. I was given instructions on healing scriptures to read daily, bible study to do and how to develop a relationship with God.*

*Because I knew that others would try to pull me back into this lifestyle, I was instructed to seek God about moving. So I moved and followed the instructions I was given. I kept in contact with the Akiens throughout the next several months. In May 2, 2009, I met the Akiens for the first time. During a session with them the truth came out for the reason of my lifestyle choice. I had been physically molested at age 5 by my older brother and then again by another relative. All these things had been blocked from my memories. I had been rejected by my mother and others. When the truth comes out, you can really be set free because the TRUTH WILL SET YOU FREE. I prayed a prayer of forgiveness for those who had hurt me and I was truly set free.*

*As I went for dialysis each day, I read my bible study during that time. My relationship with God was right and good. If I was not in my bible study, I was on the prayer line interceding for others even while I was at dialysis. After my session I even stopped overeating and liked me. For the first time, I was truly happy. I felt good and in love with God as He was in love with me. I was learning His love language. I had a real relationship like Mrs. Akiens would tell me about.*

It felt so, so, so good. Tawan's story does not end here. God called Tawan home to spend eternity with Him in December of 2009. Tawan was found dead in his apartment sitting at a table with his bible opened. The medical report stated that Tawan died of natural causes, not kidney failure. The beauty in Tawan's story is that God spoke to Tawan one day and Tawan heard His voice and responded to it. God provided a way for Tawan to get his life right and to develop a relationship with Him. God not only provided a way for Tawan's deliverance, but He provided a way for his complete healing.

Christ reconciles to God both sinners and sufferers. When Christ descended into hell, He not only brought cleansing from the guilty memories of our sins that condemn our consciences, but He also brought healing for those painful memories that arise within us to torment and enslave us. Many of our memories come from injuries and infirmities that we did not choose. We have all experienced hurts, fears, embarrassment, and unfair treatment as we have traveled along life's pathway. In many cases, we have made the adjustments necessary to get on with life and leave these inner issues hidden or buried. In some cases, the unhealthy aspects of our environment were so pervasive, or one or more experiences were so traumatic, that the lasting effects interfere with our ability to live comfortable, productive and "normal" lives. Having successful intimate relationships is a part of that as well.

    For example, I received a call from a prosecuting attorney's office concerning a 26 year old lady we will call Lady L. Lady L had been arrested for prostitution, once again. She had been warned that should she get arrested one more time, there would be criminal charges filed against her. Her case was in General Session Court and they wanted to transfer or change the charges to Criminal Court. The prosecutor then called me in to interview and counsel this young lady. My goal was to find a reason for her behavior. The prosecutor stated that the Judge had warned her not to ever get arrested again for prostitution, for she had contracted HIV.

    In my talking with her and praying for her, God revealed that her prostitution stemmed from her childhood. After counseling with Lady L it was revealed as a child she was raped by her step-father. When she approached her mother concerning this, her mother sided with the step-father and threw her out.

    The Holy Spirit revealed to me that she prostituted herself in order to spread the HIV virus to as many men as she could because of the person who gave it to her, and her way of dealing with the hurt and pain from her childhood. However, every man she slept with represented her stepfather and in her mind she was trying to kill him through every man that had sex with her. Because prostitution was illegal, it matched what her stepfather had done to her and the man that gave her HIV.

It is most important to understand that the healing of memories has a solid foundation in the Scriptures, which is our final authority in all matters of faith and practice. Those who come to Jesus from a life of sin are filled with brokenness, emotional scars, hurts, and rejection. They are bound and imprisoned to many habits and thought patterns. Many are still full of anxiety, worry, and depression. They are numb, badly crushed, and confused. When we come to Jesus, our sin of rejecting Him is forgiven. We are born again. We receive a new life, a new heart, and are taken into His Kingdom. There are still many areas in our life that have been destroyed by sin. These areas are in need of restoration and transformation by the Holy Spirit. In fact, Paul says that we are transformed. *(Romans.12:2)*

This renewing of the mind takes place in two ways. The first is by the washing of the water of the Word through having our mind bathed and saturated in the Word of Jesus daily. The second is by the inner healing restoration of the soul and the deliverance from anything to which the believer is held captive. Jesus has provided a ministry for this type of renewing by the Holy Spirit. It is found written in the Book of Isaiah the prophet. It is these Scriptures that Jesus quoted when He began His own ministry.

In *Isaiah 61:1-4"The Spirit of the Lord God is upon Me; because the Lord hath anointed Me to preach good tidings unto the meek; He hath sent Me to bind up the brokenhearted, to proclaim liberty to the captives, and the opening of the prison to them that are bound; To proclaim the acceptable year of the Lord, and the day of vengeances of our God; to comfort all that mourns; To appoint unto them that mourn in Zion, to give unto them beauty for ashes, the oil of joy for mourning, the garment of praise for the spirit of heaviness; that they might be called trees of righteousness, the planting of the Lord, that He might be glorified; And they shall build the old wastes, they shall raise up the former desolations, and they shall repair the waste cities, the desolations of many generations."*

It is this Scripture quoted that the Holy Spirit is upon us to accomplish. It is for this that He has anointed us. It is this passage that we find the basis for the ministry of inner healing and deliverance for the Body of Christ. As we study this passage, we find that there are three main areas involved in this ministry: 1. *healing of the memories* -- "Binding up the broken-hearted, setting at liberty those that are bruised." 2. *Deliverance* -- "proclaiming deliverance to captives, the opening of prison to those who are bound." 3. *Breaking and renouncing of curses which are passed down from generation to generation* -- "rising up the former devastations, repairing the desolations of many generations." (The Master's Healing Presence Bible King James Version)

When people have never faced their painful memories or been loosened (unbound) from them, they are still hung up (or suspended) at a certain age and stage of their development. Their emotions never grew beyond a certain level. At that particular point they got stuck, hung-up (or suspended); hence the term. Personality or emotional hang-ups come as a result of memories that bind and hold us in a vise-like grip. Such painful memories are like weights tied to a swimmer's body. They keep pulling us down. Thus we are just barely able to keep afloat. Until they have a picture and feel the sense that God is truly good and gracious, there can be no lasting spiritual victory in their lives.

Healing also involves letting go of guilt, shame, and/or resentment. This may involve a process of forgiveness (if and when a person is ready) and of learning to see oneself in a different light. Another aspect of letting go is accepting the truth from your inner healing and deliverance and not justifying what the Holy Spirit is revealing to you. You must learn to separate the past from the present. The painful memories of unhealthy relationships often cry out so loudly that they interfere with learning the new relationship with God. There are two things that are often necessary to correct the damage. First, a healing of the primary relationship that caused the problem. Second, we need to develop trusting relationships.

People can go through their lives reacting to certain situations and not realizing why. Back in the mind is buried a memory that is distasteful which brings the reaction. Everyone has a reason for reacting the way he does. At the heart of all remembering is association, for associations are the links that cause our minds to recall experiences.

Many of these hurts and bruises are hidden in our memory and forgotten. The only way we can know them is by the Holy Spirit. *"He reveals the deep and secret things; He knows what is in the darkness, and the light dwells with Him!"* (Daniel 2:22 Comparative Study Bible NIV/Amplified/KJV/ Updated NASB)

I remember one Saturday I was at the beauty shop setting under the hairdryer when the Holy Spirit spoke to me and stated that I had never mourned my grandmother's death. Tears started falling down my face uncontrollably. I never knew my grandmother because my mother was pregnant with me when she passed. By experiencing these feelings, the memories associated with those feelings entered my consciousness. By accepting what the Holy Spirit revealed, I was set free.

*"But, the Counselor, which is the Holy Ghost, whom the Father will send in my name, "He shall teach you all things, and bring all things to your remembrance, whatsoever I have said unto you."* (John 14:26 Comparative Study Bible NIV /Amplified /KJV/ Updated NASB)

One time early in my life, I was in class when suddenly I felt a very deep feel come up out of my belly and I started crying uncontrollably. I heard myself say "O' no God I don't want to hate anybody, no not my mother." I remember my instructor stopping class and instructing me to act like she were my mother and say everything to her that came to my mind. I couldn't do it because the pain, the hurt, and sadness started surfacing. I had no control over them. So, we placed a chair in the middle of the room and I envisioned that it was my mother. The little girl in me then began to release all the pain from that memory. Thank God that was a Christian School. The instructor stated she had been praying for God truth to be revealed in class.

The Body of Christ does not grasp that this verse means that the Counselor will enlighten our mind so that we may remember what the Lord has spoken. It instead instructs us to not to engage our memory because God shall bring all things to our minds. We accordingly allow our memory to degenerate into passivity because we do not exercise our will to remember. What is the outcome? – (a) "the man himself does not use his memory; (b) God does not use it, because He will not do so apart from the believer's co-action; (c) evil spirits use it, and substitute their workings in the place of the believer's volitional use of his memory." (Nee)

We then realize that our enemy is not our coworker, church member, Satan, or our sibling, but the enemy is self. It's the person you sleep with every day, eat with, and bathe with. It is the one that goes every place you go. It's the person who's looking back at you in the mirror. Self is trying to get you to self-destruct. It's all the hurt, pain, unforgiveness, resentment, bitterness, anger, and rage. It's every hurtfully thing you have experienced in your life. It's the hurt from your mother or father and how they treated you as a child. It's the feeling of being unloved, unwanted, unappreciated, unneeded, or being rejected by some other person in your life. It's everything you thought someone did do to you. It's the bad marriage or divorce. It's when you wanted that person to like you and instead, they made fun of you. It's that feeling of loneliness or depression. It's every lie that we have believed that's contrary to what and who God says that we are. God created us in His image, not what our situation has tried to dictate to us. God is Holy and we were created to have the same attributes, or characteristics of God.

      When the Body of Christ understands the truth about who they truly are, they understand their authority, power, and rights. They begin to understand that their inner self is working against them and self is the one that has given their Adversary the right to wreak havoc in their life. If you don't forgive, he has the right to be there. Yes most of these things you did not have control over at first, but now that we have accepted Jesus as our Lord and Savior, we are supposed to seek Him in spirit and in truth. The word of God states that when he, the Spirit of truth comes, will guide (reveal) us into all truth. Who the Son makes free is free indeed. We should accept what the Father is trying to reveal as truth even if we do not understand it at first. Most of the time, a justifying part of the inner self will try to justify what God is revealing to you.

## Chapter 6

## What Is Your Shame?

Christ identified with us in our shame and bore it away so that our personal dignity could be restored. If you have ever been shamed, embarrassed, made to feel worthless, or degraded, then you need to read this.

Nelson's Illustrated Bible Dictionary [1] gives this definition: SHAME -- *A negative emotion caused by an awareness of wrongdoing, hurt ego, or guilt.* In the Bible, the feeling of shame is normally caused by public exposure of one's guilt. (Genesis 2:25; 3:10) Shame may also be caused by a hurt reputation or embarrassment, whether or not this feeling is due to sin. (Psalm 25:2-3; Proverbs 19:26; Romans 1:16)

Joseph, not wishing to shame Mary, desired to divorce her secretly. (Matthew 1:19) Our Lord Jesus suffered the shame of the Cross because He was put on public display as the recipient of God's wrath. (2 Corinthians 5:21; Hebrews 12:2)

According to this Bible dictionary, shame is caused by one of two ways: either the awareness or exposure of guilt, or a hurt reputation or embarrassment; whether or not this feeling is due to sin. Shame is also caused by being wronged, abused, or mistreated when one's personal rights are violated. This could occur a number of ways, but the most vivid example I know of is when a child is verbally, physically, or sexually abused by an adult. The shame received by such abuse can be lifelong and far reaching.

## How Does Shame Affect You?

Think back over your life to a time when you were shamed. Perhaps a parent disciplined you publicly and other children teased you about it. Maybe you were falsely accused of cheating in school and unjustly punished. Perhaps your reputation was marred in some way and you had to live it down. Maybe you did something wrong, but were improperly corrected and have carried the embarrassment of your actions ever since. Here are some important facts about shame which have been verified through many fields of study:

**1. A loss of dignity.**
Each individual is born with a sense of *personhood;* which, if properly nurtured, will instinctively help him or her make the right life choices. There are many unbelievers who are basically moral people due to the fact they have chosen to keep their dignity and were fortunate enough to avoid abuse during their formative years. Some, however, were needlessly shamed in early life and grew up with a sense of loss about their personhood. There are too many ways this can happen to list here, but a few are:

    If a father really wanted a son but got a girl, he can unknowingly damage her sense of personhood by treating her like a boy and shaming her when she acts like a little girl. There are many masculine women in our society whose personhood was not properly nurtured during childhood. "Daddy's tomboy" for a girl is not any more healthy than "Mommy's little girl" for a boy!

Another way children are shamed is when they are told they are stupid, dumb, etc. When adolescents go through a clumsy stage, it is easy during those tender, vulnerable years, to degrade their sense of personal value through family members calling them names, even in times of humor. The gangly teen may laugh along with the rest of the family, but is often crying inside.

Adopted children are sometimes stigmatized by our society. They grow up with a spirit of rejection, feeling unwanted, unneeded, unloved, or illegitimate. Even as adults, they often feel loss because they do not know their biological parents and go to great lengths to find them.

When children are punished in anger or punished in the wrong way, (slapping in the face, etc.) their personal dignity is demolished by the authority figure in their lives which can cause them to incorrectly surmise that God thinks they have little value, too. A damaged person is often tempted to doubt God's ability to restore from guilt and shame. God encourages all who were shamed in their childhood, however, that **"Thou shall forget the shame of thy youth." (Isaiah 54:4)**

Adults can be shamed too; through divorce, failure, rape, bankruptcy, or other traumas. There are hosts of ways a person can be shamed. Ask our Father to show you how you have been degraded by your life experiences. However your dignity may have suffered, or your personhood destroyed, you need to realize that part of the work of God in your life is to restore you to wholeness in which He created you to be.

## 2. Produces emotional pain.

When a person is shamed, his or her emotions are damaged. This causes a sense of loss, hurt, and devaluation. The macho mentality refuses to acknowledge the reality of emotional pain, boasting that "Sticks and stones may break my bones, but words will never hurt me." God's Word, however, teaches that words can injure the innermost part of a person. **(Proverbs 18:8)** Unlike broken skin though, a broken spirit does not automatically heal.

Emotional pain can be so real that it can actually cause physical pain such as heaviness in the chest, upset of the digestive process, headaches, and sleep disturbances. Sometimes there is a physical pain which is based solely in the emotions.

## 3. Shamed people medicate their pain.

The Body of Christ lick their emotional wounds by *medicating their pain* through a multitude of means: sports, food, money, sex, television, personal achievements, immoral relationships, drugs, alcohol, tobacco, rage and pornography, and various other things. Some of them in themselves are not wrong, (take food for instance) but we abuse them by over indulgence in an attempt to medicate our pain. In the thorough book, **Love Hunger,** the doctors of the Minirth-Meier clinic spell out reasons why we overeat and show how, in most cases, a person is actually attempting to fill a hole inside.

Many hurting people turn to the church in an effort to alleviate the pain they feel. After being involved for a while, they often drop out and are still hurting. Some people use religion to evade their pain and deny their true feelings. Church is an escape to them like theater is to someone else.

Pain calls for alleviation. If the alleviation itself is sinful, then the individual feels guilt which produces more shame-pain. This in turn calls for more of the addictive substance or practice, and so the cycle goes. This is how a person, or a society, becomes compulsive and addicted.

**Our Substitute**

Jesus Christ is alive today and able to meet our deepest needs so that these next years will witness a revolutionary healing in the deep cores of hurting people. They will no longer need to medicate pain because their gut feelings will be healed and their compulsions will be forgotten in the light of His grace! Jesus is not only our *Guilt Offering*, but our Shame Bearer.

**How Did Jesus Bear Our Shame?**

All His sufferings on our behalf, in a general sense, were for our shame when the Messiah was publicly beaten, mocked, whipped, and nailed to the Cross. In a specific sense, however, Jesus bore our shame in several distinct ways. These ways include when He was spit upon, beat publicly, when they marched Him publicly, and when He was nailed to the cross. The cross was the worst form of humiliation and shame.

## Shame by Spitting

In the Old Testament, spitting in the face was a gesture of contempt and a deliberate insult. Job, during his trial, was such an object of disgrace that people spat upon him in disgust. (Job 30:10) He not only lost his children, his wealth, and his health, but he lost his honor, too. For that, the people expressed themselves by spitting on the poor fellow as they walked by.

Miriam, after criticizing Moses about his wife, was smitten with leprosy. Moses prayed for God to miraculously heal her rather than having her wait throughout a seclusion period. He demanded a cure for leprosy in the Levitical laws. (Leviticus 13, 14) The Lord answered him, "If her father had but spit in her face, should she not be ashamed seven days? Let her be shut out from the camp seven days, and after that let her be received in again." (Numbers 12:14)

In this scripture, we see reference to the accepted custom of a father spitting on his daughter for behaving foolishly. The daughter would be publicly disgraced, though not disowned, by her father's public spittle. After a period of humiliation and isolation, she would be welcomed back to her family. If this seems harsh, and it was, just remember that a son who behaved foolishly could be brought to the city's gate and stoned! (Deuteronomy 21:18-21)

**They Shall Spit Upon Him**

The key thought is that many ancient peoples, not only Hebrews, *expressed shame by spitting.* Jesus Christ was spat upon during the course of His vicarious sufferings. (Matthew 27:30; Mark 15:19) He foretold this would happen two different times: when He was on earth, (Mark 10:34; Luke 18:32) and centuries before He became flesh. The Word spoke through Isaiah, **"I gave My back to the smiters, and my cheeks to them that plucked off the hair: I hid not My face from SHAME AND SPITTING."** (Isaiah 50:6)

Notice how the phrase "shame and spitting" goes together in Isaiah's prophecy. Jesus actually bore our shame when He was spit upon so we could be emotionally healed of shame and disgrace! Christ was mocked, devalued, jeered, and mistreated on our behalf.

**Have You Ever Been Despised?**

Think back over the course of your life. Can you remember times when your sense of value was cheapened by the behavior of others? If they were your authority figures, did you accept the unkind remarks they made about you as true of yourself? Have you ever said the same type of things others said long ago about you? If you answer yes to any of these questions, then you may be living in a very real sense of shame.

Jesus Christ made those He contacted feel better about themselves. Even an adulteress walked away with her sense of worth restored. (John 8) Isaiah predicted that the Messiah would be

**"...despised and rejected of men".** Spurgeon commented, "...So the reader need not bear it." (Isaiah 53:3) Christ bore the emotional ills of His people so we would not have to medicate our pain. Instead, we can believe that He **"...carried our sorrows"** for us. **(Isaiah 53:4)** (Nelson's Illustrated Bible Dictionary)

## Chapter 7

## Fear

Webster's dictionary says that fear is "to...expect with alarm." (Webster's II) Now, as Christians, we are supposed to have a sense of expectancy. However, a person who is experiencing fear lays in wait for what seems to be an unavoidable catastrophe. I have a strange feeling that this is not the kind of expectancy God had in mind. One of my favorite definitions of fear is **F**alse **E**vidence **A**ppearing **R**eal. In our mind's eye, the false fears can sometimes seem more real than anything else around us. *"For God did not give us a spirit of fearfulness (of cowardice, of craven and cringing and fawning fear), but (He has given us a spirit) one of power, love, and sound judgment (of a calm and well-balanced mind and discipline and self-control)"* (2 Timothy 1:7) (Holman Illustrated Study Bible)

There are a few important points that this scripture brings up.
1. **Fear is a spirit.**
2. **It is a spirit that God did not give to us.**
3. **Are self-discipline, self-control, and love are our protection from fear?**

Fear is a spirit and it is a spirit that does not come from God. Fear is a spirit of torment sent out by our enemy, the devil. However, we should not be surprised. The Bible says that "we are not fighting against flesh-and-blood enemies, but against evil rulers and authorities of the unseen world...and against evil spirits in the heavenly places."

(Ephesians 6:12) God says that Satan only comes to "steal, kill, and to destroy." (John 10:10) The spirit of fear is sent out to do those things. Fear is, quite plainly, a spiritual attack designed not only to steal your peace, but your destiny in Christ. An excellent example of this is what happened to Peter in Matthew 14. He was on the edge of greatness, but his fear stole his miracle.

"About three o'clock in the morning Jesus came toward them, walking on the water... Then Peter called to Him, "Lord, if it's really you, tell me to come to you, walking on the water." "Yes come," Jesus said. So Peter went over the side of the boat and **walked on the water** toward Jesus. However, when he saw the strong wind and the waves, **he was terrified and began to sink** Jesus immediately reached out and grabbed him. "You of little faith..." Jesus said. **"Why did you doubt?"** (Matthew 14:25, 28-31 Comparative Study Bible NIV /Amplified /KJV/ Updated NASB)

God says He did not give us a spirit of fear, *"but of power, love, and of a calm and well-balanced mind of discipline and self-control."* When we are afraid, our minds are not well-balanced, as God describes. When we fear or doubt God, we are said to be double minded. (James 1:8) God says that when a person comes to Him, *"it must be in faith that he asks with no wavering (no hesitating, no doubting)....For truly, let not such a person imagine that He will receive anything (he asks for) from the Lord, (For being as he is) a man of two minds (hesitating, dubious, irresolute), (he is) unstable and unreliable and uncertain about everything (he thinks, feels, decide.)* (James 1:6-8) (Comparative Study Bible NIV/Amplified/KJV/ Updated NASB)

That is exactly what the spirit of fear wants to do to us. It wants to make us unstable, unreliable, and uncertain about everything such as our thoughts and God's promises. Anyone who has ever been afraid can attest to the truth of that scripture. Why our fear is double minded? Part of our mind may believe God's promises of love and provision, but our doubts and fears reveal hidden beliefs contrary to those promises. **You can't believe Jehovah Rappha is your healer, and then fear you'll die of cancer. You can't believe Jehovah Jireh is your provider, and then fear you'll go bankrupt.** That is being double minded.

Imagine if your children had that much doubt in your **desire** or **ability** to care for them. That is why God says that a double minded person should not expect to receive anything from Him because you don't have to be double minded, unstable, and uncertain. You can have God's peace and learn how to faith your fears to death! Faith and fear are very similar in nature. Both faith and fear are an unshakable belief in an unseen future. Neither is merely emotional, but both are spiritual forces.

The only difference between the two is that one believes God will come through for you, and the other believes He won't. God says that He has not given us the spirit of fear, but that He has given us love, power, and self-control (2 Timothy 1:7). They are our most powerful weapons in our battle for freedom as we master controlling emotions of fear, doubt, and worry. God's power is living inside of us, and He has given us the power to stand against the enemy's attacks. *"Be strong in the Lord and in His mighty power"*. *"Put on the whole armor of God, that ye may be able to stand against the wiles of the devil. For we wrestle against flesh-and-blood, but against principalities, against powers, against the rulers of the darkness of this world, against spiritual wickedness in the heavenly places. Wherefore, take unto you the whole armor of God that ye may be able to withstand in the evil day, and having done all, to stand."* (Ephesians 6:10-13) (Hebrew-Greek)

How do you begin controlling emotions and thoughts? We fill our mind with the promises of God. One of the best ways to safeguard our mind against the emotional attacks of the enemy is by meditating on God's Word on a regular basis. That takes self-discipline! Whether we realize it or not, everyone meditates. The true meaning of meditation is to roll a thought over in your mind, over and over again. The issue that most Christians have is not that they do not know how to meditate, but that they are meditating on their problems and not their promises. They do not discipline their minds as God has instructed us to.

*"For the weapons of our warfare are not physical (weapons of flesh and blood), but they are mighty before God for the overthrow and destruction of strongholds, (Inasmuch as we) refute arguments and theories and reasoning's and every proud and lofty thing that sets itself up against the (true) knowledge of God; and we lead every thought and purpose away captive into the obedience of Christ the Messiah, the Anointed On."* (2 Corinthians 10:4-

5 AMP Comparative Study Bible NIV /Amplified/KJV/ Updated NASB)

The more that we discipline ourselves to meditate on God's Word, the easier it will become to reject thoughts that don't line up with it. That's what fears are; thoughts that do not line up with God's promises to you. Fear says God will not help you this time. Fear says your children won't come back to the Lord. Fear says that your finance will never improve. Fear says that your marriage is ruined. Fear says the opposite of what God says. When a fear creeps up inside of you, it should be a red flag that you need to continue deepening your relationship with God. How do you begin controlling emotions of fear, doubt, and worry? Our faith in the unyielding love of your Heavenly Father is what removes fear from your mind, regardless of your circumstances. God has promised that *"For I know the plans I have for you," declares the* LORD, *plans for welfare and not for calamity to give you a future and a hope."* (Jeremiah 29:1 Comparative Study Bible NIV/Amplified/KJV/ Updated NASB)

God has made out plans for our life just like any good parent, because He loves us. However, he is unlike any earthly parent because He has the power to bring those plans to pass. Knowing that small piece of truth can help us overcome fear in a big way. That does not mean that the spirit of fear will never try to attack us. It means that your shield of faith can become strong enough to resist it. Next time you feel yourself starting to worry, follow these simple steps for controlling emotions of fear.

**5 Steps to Controlling Fear**
1. Recognize the fearful thought as a threat.
2. Think of God's promise for that situation. (If you don't know what it is, find out!)
3. Pray and tell God your concern.
4. Praise God for His promise to provide your needs.
5. Refuse to worry about it anymore. If it comes to your mind again, confess that you have given it over to your Heavenly Father in prayer. Begin praising God that He heard your prayers and that the prayers of the righteous availeth much. (James 5:16)

Fear is something that does not discriminate, for it affects men, women, children, and adults. At some point in our lives, we all have to come face to face with it, and the Body of Christ is no exceptions. Fear is a crippling feeling that infiltrates the mind, thus dictating emotional, intellectual, physical, and spiritual activity. Though we are talking about controlling emotions, fear is much more than *just* an emotion. (just as most emotions are) Franklin D. Roosevelt once proclaimed, "The Only Thing We Have to Fear Is Fear Itself!"

Why should we *fear* fear? We should *fear* fear because fear is a thief. It starts out by stealing God's peace from our hearts. If we let it paralyze us from action, it can rob us of our true destinies in Christ. As a Christian, fear should be our enemy. The choice between faith and fear is an easy one to make, but can be a hard one to keep! However, God has given us special weapons to use in this spiritual battle. Fear does not believe in what God has promised to His children through His word. I have been one who lived in fear. When I use to go to sleep at night, I feared that I was going to die and not know it. I use to wake up screaming and hollering from this awful feeling. I used to fear people, but God has healed that area of my life. I found out as I was reading "Fear is Never Your Friend", that I had to deal with fear about writing papers. I never knew that until God showed me that that was a problem.

    I know that the opposite of faith is fear. I have read and heard sermons on this; as well as even reasoned this in my mind. However, when fear grips, it takes over and there is no attempt to put in place the fear faith principle. I say this to illustrate that it is not a heartfelt attitude, but something that I have to remind myself of. There is no automatic response to extinguish our fear. Fear is something that starts as early as from childhood, and can be passed on from in the womb. I feel that there are people who will feed our Christian fear by not believing in us and second guessing decisions we have made. This causes us to fear, doubt, and turn from our decisions. While sometimes this is wise and good, sometimes it is not. God hath not given us the spirit of fear, but of power, love, and sound mind. This scripture verse was one of the first I learned in hopes of renewing my mind and learning to bring every thought captive to the obedience of Christ. (Richardson, Fear is Never Your Friend)

## Chapter 8

## Hurt People, Hurt People

It is an old adage that says "hurt people hurt people." It is well known that those who have been emotionally damaged tend to inflict their hurt and pain on other people. For example, a large percentage of those who have been sexually abused become the abusers of others. Those who suffered under an alcoholic parent often themselves cause their future family to suffer because of their drunken stupors. Until we as the Body of Christ deals with the whole person as shown in 1 Thessalonians 5:23, our congregations will be filled with people who are spiritually gifted, but act like emotional infants. In other words, the Body of Christ must deal with emotional health and not just spiritual health and power.

**The following are common traits hurt people display in their interactions with others.**

**I. Hurt people often transfer their inner anger onto their family and close friends.**

 *Often those around them become the recipients of harsh tones and fits of rage because they have unknowingly become the vicarious recipients of transferred rage.

**II. Hurt people interpret every word spoken to them through the prism of their pain.**

 * Because of their pain, ordinary words are often misinterpreted to mean something negative towards

them.

* Because of this, they are extremely sensitive and act out of pain instead of reality.

### III. Hurt people interpret every action through the prism of their pain.

* Their emotional pain causes them to suspect wrong motives or evil intent behind other people's actions towards them.

### IV. Hurt people often portray themselves as victims and carry a "victim spirit".

* Often hurt people can cry sexism, homophobia, or often use the words unjust and unfair to describe the way they are being treated, even if there is no truth to this. (That is not to say that sometimes there really is sexism in some instances. This is just used as an example.)

* Hurt people have a hard time entering into a trusting relationship.

* Hurt people often carry around a suspicious spirit.

### V. Hurt people often alienate others and wonder why no one is there for them.

* They often continually hurt the ones they love and need the most with their self-destructive behavior.

### VI. Hurt people have the emotional maturity of the age they received their (un-dealt with) hurt.

* For example, if a girl was raped by a man when she was 12 years old, unless she forgives that man and allows Christ to heal her heart and allay her fears, in that particular area of her life, (sexuality

with a man) her emotional growth will stop. Even when she reaches her later years, she may still have the emotional maturity of a 12 year-old. Example: The Program Manger of a probation company that I sometime worked for called me and requested that I interview a young man who was on probation as a sex offender. The young man had stated to his probation officer on one of his visits that something was trying to make him commit another act, and that he did not want to do this, but something was trying to force him.

During the interview process it was revealed to me by the Holy Spirit that this man had been raped as a child. When I asked him "who raped you?" he began to cry. It also came out that he was not just a "sex offender", but also a pedophile. He stated he did not want to do it, but something was making him do it. I asked him about his relationship with God. I counseled him about unforgiveness. He went through the prayer of repentance and God revealed names to him of people that had hurt him who he needed to forgive. Then God revealed to him the names of the people he had hurt and he repented. He forgave everyone who had hurt him as a child and throughout his past. This young man would not forgive the person who raped him as a child. He stated he could never forgive that person. Without complete forgiveness of all who have hurt you in your past, there cannot be complete deliverance and healing.

VII. **Hurt people are often frustrated and depressed because past pain continually spills over into their present consciousness.**

.* In many instances, they may not even be aware of why they are continually frustrated or depressed because they have coped with pain by compartmentalizing it or layering it over with other things over time.

VIII. **Hurt people often erupt with inappropriate emotion because particular words, actions, or circumstances "touch" and "trigger" past wounds.**

IX. **Hurt people often occupy themselves with busyness, work, performance, and/or accomplishments as a way of compensating for low self-esteem.**
* Often, ministers are not motivated by a love for Jesus, but a drive to accomplish.
* It is important that pastors and ministers be led by the Spirit instead of being driven to succeed.
* A minister should not preoccupy himself with making things happen. He/she should walk with integrity and humility, and allow God to open up doors and provide a ministerial platform according to their assignment for their life and ministry.

X. **Hurt people often attempt to medicate themselves with excessive entertainment, drugs, alcohol, pornography, sexual relationships, or hobbies as a way to forget their pain and run from reality.**
* Until the Body of Christ learns to deal with and emphasize the emotional life and health of the believer, the church will be filled with half-

Christians who pray and read the Bible, but find no victory because they do not face the wounds within their souls.

XI. **Hurt people have learned to accommodate their private "false self" or "dark side", which causes them to be duplicitous and lack integrity.**
* Often their private life is different from their public life, which causes hypocrisy and compounds feelings of guilt, condemnation, and depression.

XII. **Hurt people are often self-absorbed with their own pain and are unaware that they are hurting other people.**
* They are often insensitive to other people because their emotional pain limits their capacity for empathy and self-awareness.
* I have been in several situations when someone hurt me and kept on going in the relationship without ever apologizing because they had no clue what they were doing.

XIII. **Hurt people are susceptible to demonic deception.**
* I am convinced that most of the divisions in the church are caused by saints who lack emotional health and project their pain onto others.
* Satan works in darkness and deception, staying away from the light. Hurt people often have destructive habit-patterns that are practiced in the dark. Hence, their mind becomes a breeding ground for satanic infiltration and deception.

* If the church would deal more with the emotional health of the individual, there would be less of a foothold for demonic infiltration. There would be stronger relationships, marriages, healthier children, and a more balanced approach to ministry with less of a chance of pastoral and congregational burnout.

### XIV. God often purposely surfaces pain so hurt people can face reality.

* Whether it is because of a marriage problem, or continual personal conflicts on the job, God often allows conflict and spillover because he wants the infection to stop spreading and the person to be healed.

* Often Christians are fighting the devil and blaming him for conflict when in essence, God often allows conflict so that people would be motivated to dig deeper into their lives to deal with root causes of destructive thought and habit patterns.

* God's purpose for us is that we would all be conformed to the image of Christ. (Romans 8:29) This does not just happen with Bible studies, prayer, and times of glory, but also in painful situations when we have to face what has been hurting us for many years.

### XV. Hurt people need to forgive to be released and restored to freedom.

* The Gospel of St. John 20:23 says that we have to release the sins of others if we are going to be released. This means that if we do not forgive others, then the very thing we have become victimized with will become a part of our life. For example, alcoholic

fathers breed alcoholic sons if their sons do not forgive and release their fathers.

## Chapter 9

## Wounded Heart

The heart or the spirit is the source of our life. It is the center of our being. If the spirit is damaged, wounded, or corrupted in any way, (and the Bible says it can be) our ability to relate normally to others, ourselves, and to God is hampered. *"Keep and guard your heart with all vigilance and above all that you guard (your heart), for out of it flows the springs of life."* (Proverbs 4:23) (Comparative Study Bible NIV/Amplified/KJV/ Updated NASB)

Jesus said in Luke 4:18-19, quoting Isaiah, *"The Spirit of the Lord is upon me, because he has anointed me to preach the gospel to the poor; he has sent me to heal the brokenhearted, to preach deliverance to the captives, and recovering of sight to the blind, to set at liberty them that are bruised, to preach the acceptable year of the Lord."* (Holy Bible King James Version)

Dr. David Allen, in Search of the Heart states that "You can become a missionary to your own heart if you have suffered hurts to your heart, as we all have. Dr. Allen expresses that you need to clear out the pain, hurt, and anger of past experiences, and free your heart of feelings that hold it captive. Discover your authentic self by confronting your false self, the image you allow others to see. Finally, rediscover the loving and life-affirming experiences in your life that have been blocked by painful emotions." (Allen)

A person with a wounded spirit lives in **inner hurt** that focuses regularly on **his injuries** or **pain**, and cannot receive the cleansing. Usually, there is unforgiveness and self-pity in a wounded heart. Unforgiveness and self-pity are the glue that holds you to the pain of your past.

Have you met people that no matter how hard they try to walk, seem to fall? One day they have faith, and the next day they have doubt and unbelief? That's because they have a broken heart and cannot stand. You can tell them to stand on the word and quote promises, but they cannot. That is because they have a broken heart!

Someone with a broken heart has pain and hurt that never goes away! Time will not bring complete healing to them. **They do not understand**. Whenever they remember the experience, they feel the hurt. Some people will even block out their memory so that they won't have to face feeling the hurts, but they are still there.

See, King David heart was hurt when he cried out *"Create in me a clean heart, O God; and renew a right spirit within me."* (Psalm 51:10) (Holy Bible King James Version) You were just like King David the moment you asked God to forgive you of your sins. God created a clean heart in you and He renewed a right spirit within you. That's exactly what happens for you and what happened to King David once he reached that moment of repentance. (Bynum)

It is your "old mind" that keeps you functioning outside of the will of God. That's why the Word states in Romans 12:2 *"Do not be conformed to this world...*" Your mind needs to constantly be renewed day by day because it's a process. Just like a new job, you have to meet the qualifications, learn the policy and procedures, and also learn the do's and don'ts. Every day you learn something new about your new position requirement. You renew your mind every day to this new position. There are things from your old job and position that you are not able to do at your new job. You have to **conform** to their company policy and procedures. Not only do you change jobs, but you change "**your boss**", who you answer to.

      For example, let's say you have two jobs and you have to be at your primary one at 8:00 a.m. – 4:30 p.m. Monday thru Friday, and the second one at 5:30 p.m. until 10:30 p.m. However, the second job calls and asks you to come in at 8:00 a.m., knowing that you are supposed to be at your primary job. They tell you they would double your pay if you come in. Now you have to make the decision on whether to take the money or not. Your **boss** just became that money, not what was right, and you were supposed to be at work with your primary job. When you come to God, you change your boss from Satan to Him. You change who you work for. (Holy Bible King James Version)

      It is your choice if your renewed mind does not come into harmony with your heart. Only you can choose whether to follow the stubborn habits that are stored in your memories, or submit to the wisdom that flows out of your new heart. Dr. Bynum stated in Matters of the Heart, "It's so important to have a new heart and to know that you have it." (Bynum)

So many people go to church week after week thinking that just because they go to church and are the pastor, deacon, elder, praise leaders, greeter, or minister that they've got it all together. However, their heart is not right. I remember at one church, God told me to look at the people in the congregation. He stated that when they were in the world they did everything that they were big and bad enough to do. When they decided to give their life to Him, they walked down the church aisle and got the right hand to the fellowship of the church. Then, He asked what does that mean? Before I could answer Him, He stated they got the rights to the church (to that building). He told me no one is getting them to repent for their sins against Him. Therefore, they are working in the church in right fellow with them, but are out of right relationship with Him.

I remember we had this lady at church that had this saying she use to say if she approved of you. Everyone knew that if she said "Plum Rich, Just Plum Rich", she approved of them. That was here seal of approval. She got sick and I was part of a sick and shut in ministry. We were going to pray for her, but every time we scheduled a time different things would happen so that we could never go together. So, one Tuesday God told me to go. I was very reluctant, but I was obedience. When I got there she told me come on in and read the Bible to her. I heard these words come out of my mouth "no you know the bible I came to pray for you". In prayer I prayed a prayer of repentance, forgiveness, and everything that God gave me for her. God brought back to her remembrance that she had some unforgiveness in her heart and that she had put her mouth on some of His children. I lead her to ask God with a sincere heart to forgive her for all her iniquities and transgressions. I lead her to ask for forgiveness for having unforgiveness in her heart and for putting her mouth on His children. I also led her to thank Him for loving her so much that He searched her heart and brought these things to her memories.

When we were finished, God told me to not embarrass her, but give her instruction on how to call out every name that He brought to her conscience. He stated she would do it. When I finished she had tears in her eyes and running down her face. She looked at me and called who I believed to be her niece from the other room to ask her did she hear the powerful prayer. She stated yes, and then she looked at me and said "Plum Rich, Just Plum Rich".

After I left, God told me "See, you had to be the one to pray for her." The Sick and Shut in Ministry couldn't because she had had her mouth on me. She felt like God did not call me and she questioned who I was and the anointing that had been placed upon my life! He said, "So I used you to help set her free. She had been in the church all those years and never repented." This was only shared with the other ministers with the Sick and Shut in Ministry. On Tuesday of the next week, God called her home. "Now that was Just Plum Rich".

The heart can become broken or hurt by words. "Sticks and stones may break my bones, but words will never hurt me" is a dangerous lie.

*"Tongue has power of life and death, and those who love it will eat its fruit."* (Proverbs 18:21) (Comparative Study Bible NIV/Amplified/KJV/ Updated NASB)

Words have spiritual values. They create life in our spirit or they can produce death. *"A lying tongue hates those it hurts, and a flattering mouth works ruin."* (Proverbs 26:28) (Comparative Study Bible NIV/Amplified/KJV/ Updated NASB) Negativity and criticism can do more to wound and bruise the spirit than physical violence. "The tongue that brings healing is a tree of life but a deceitful tongue crushes the spirit." (Proverbs 15:4) (Comparative Study Bible NIV/Amplified/KJV/ Updated NASB)

Verbal abuse is a sad part of society. It's common to hear people making fun of and ridiculing children, spouses, and one another. In spite of the intention, this still hurts. It is particularly harmful when it comes from those who are close to us; the one's we expect support from. *"Scorn has broken my heart and has left me helpless. I looked for sympathy, but there was none, for comforters, but I found none."* (Psalm 69:20) (Comparative Study Bible NIV/Amplified/KJV/ Updated NASB)

Sexual abuse, rape, and incest are also major problems within our society. Because of the intimate nature of these forms of abuse, they are frequently concealed or denied. As a consequence, the victims are denied justice and the guilty escape blame. To hide such abuses is debasing to the victims. In Samuel, the story is told of how Amnon, the son of David, became infatuated with his half-sister Tamar and raped her. In spite of her protestations, her brother, Absalom, convinced her to conceal the assault. In times of abuse there is a great need for support. If this is not forthcoming, there is a strong sense of isolation. Without this support, those who are not at fault frequently end up blaming themselves, languishing in guilt that rightfully belongs to others. It can also be the result of an inability to forgive and let go of those who have sinned against us.

A wounded spirit is like a big sore risen just waiting for someone to prick it with a sharp word. Out of it comes all of the corruption of unforgiveness, resentment, retaliation, anger/wrath, hatred, violence, murder with the tongue, fear, rejection of others, self, and even God. Other people respond by immediately striking back trying to balance their hurt with anger and revenge or by trying to protect themselves from further hurt. However, scar tissue (hardness of heart) soon appears. A wounded heart that doesn't receive healing is an open door for evil spirits. (Ephesians 4:26-27, I Peter 5:8, Genesis 4:4-7, Matthew 18:21-35) Could you have a broken heart? Has anyone ever told you that you have a broken heart? Do you want your heart healed so that you can follow God!

## Chapter 10

## Combination Code

All the steps that we are taking by speaking words of Truth and striving to manifest the light that we have already received are carrying us on swiftly to the time when we shall have consciously the perfect mind of Christ. This comes with all the love, beauty, health, and power which that implies.

    We need not be anxious or in a hurry for the full manifestation. Let us not at any time lose sight of the fact that our desire, great as it is, is only God's desire in us. *"No one can come to me, unless drawn by the Father who sent me."* (John. 6:44) The Father in us desires to reveal to us the secret of His presence; else we had not known any hunger for the secret or for Truth. *"You did not choose me but I chose you and appointed you that you would to go and bear fruit."* (John 15:16) (Comparative Study Bible NIV/Amplified/KJV/ Updated NASB)

    After all our beating about the bush and seeking here and there for our heart's desire, we must come right to Him who is the fulfillment of every desire, who waits to manifest more of Himself to us and through us. If you wanted my love or anything that I am (not that I *have*), you would not go to Tom Jones or to Mary Smith to get it. Either of these persons might tell you that I could and would give myself, but you would have to come directly to me and receive of me that which only I am, because I am it. There is not a single key that unlocks the mystery of one's life issues, but a combination code that uncovers the secret to opening each person's door of bondage that allows them to be set free. Each part of the combination has to be identified and dealt with through acknowledging and accepting the truth about one's self. Failure to acknowledge and accept the truth on any level prohibits a complete and successful breakthrough. These symptoms are indications of inner conflicts between your inner self and outer self. Compulsions and addictions are attempts to keep one's inner self hidden from others and from one's own conscious awareness. Depression, anxiety, anger, fears, and relationship problems are all signals hidden and unconscious issues that emanate from the inner person that interfere with the effective, healthy, functioning of the outer self.

Everyone has an inner self or person, and God's plan for human development was for everyone to experience emotional nurturing during his or her formative years. This would allow the individual to grow to into a healthy adulthood, with good balance between the inner and outer dimensions of his or her personality. God has made an enormous investment in every person's inner self, with the plan that the experiences of the inner self would shape the adult personality in positive ways. Unfortunately many of our childhood experiences are negative experiences, and they result in negative influences on who we are and how we feel as adults.

The human mind is made up of both conscious and unconscious components. Your childhood experiences have a powerful influence in shaping both the conscious and unconscious aspects of who you are. There is a continual conflict between these two dimensions of your being. The unconscious mind attempts to push thoughts and memories into your conscious awareness, and your defense mechanisms fight like mad to keep the most painful and frightening of those thoughts and memories suppressed.

The inner self is the essential you that existed before you began to acquire your roles and identities as son or daughter, student, athlete, dancer, artist, nurse, doctor, friend, husband, wife, parent, or career person. Before any of these identities were added to you, there was a basic, essential you. When you were born, you were nothing but a naked inner child without any outer self at all. You were innocent, curing, naïve, uninhibited, spontaneous, and totally vulnerable. You had no defense, no facades, and no image to project.

As you grew, you learned social norms, behavioral expectations, and ways to manipulate your environment. You learned that in order to avoid pain or shame, you should keep certain parts of your inner self hidden from others. You learned that other people would accept or reject you on the basis of things you said and did, so you began to monitor and adjust your behavior to the expectation of others.

In the book of Romans, Paul urges us to change the way we think because it can transform us. "Don't copy the behavior and customs of this world, but let God transform us into a new person by changing the way we think. Then we will learn to know God's will for us, which is good and pleasing and perfect." (Romans 12:2) Finally, the writer of

Proverbs 14:30 says "A peaceful heart leads to a healthy body; jealousy is like cancer in the bones." The effect of thinking thoughts that are positive can lead to a heart at peace, which is good for the body.

We should first ask God to help us through the power that His Holy Spirit provides. He can help us change our thought life. We need to know that our true identity is in Jesus Christ, and not in what others may have told us or what the Devil may be trying to tell us through his lies. *"For the weapons of our warfare are not carnal, but mighty through God to the pulling down of strong holds"; "Casting down imaginations, and every high thing that exalteth itself against the knowledge of God and bringing into captivity every thought to the obedience of Christ."* (II Corinthians 10:4-5) (Holy Bible King James Version)

## Chapter 11

## Deliverance

What are you in bondage to? In Luke 4:18 Jesus said, *"The Spirit of the Lord is upon me, because he hath anointed me to preach the gospel to the poor; he hath sent me to heal the brokenhearted, to preach deliverance to the captives... to set at liberty them that are bruised."* By definition, deliverance is either the act of delivering someone or it is the state of being delivered. *"Now the Lord is that Spirit: and where the Spirit of the Lord is, there is liberty.* (freedom)" (2Corinthians 3:17) (Comparative Study Bible NIV/Amplified/KJV/ Updated NASB)

The worst form and type of bondage is that of being demon possessed, like the demoniac of the Gadarenes in Mark 5; but there are many other types of bondages, all of which the Lord Jesus came to set us free from. Know that God doesn't want us to be in bondage to anything or anyone. In **Luke 11:20** Jesus said, *"if I with the finger of God cast out devils, no doubt the kingdom of God is come upon you."* (Comparative Study Bible NIV /Amplified/KJV/ Updated NASB)

The gospel is the gospel of the kingdom, His kingdom. If there is no kingdom of the Lord Jesus Christ, then there is NO true gospel, but one watered down without power to change lives. Your life will only be changed when it comes under His Lordship.

*"Know ye not, that to whom ye yield yourselves servants to obey, his servants ye are to whom ye obey; whether of sin unto death, or of*

*obedience unto righteousness?"* (Romans 6:16) Romans 6:18 states *"Being then made free from sin, ye became the servants of righteousness."* (Holy Bible King James Version) If you yield yourself to sin, to the influence of evil one, then you place yourself under his authority and he will have control in your life.

In Spiritual Authority it states that "Vindication or defense or whatever reaction there may be should come from God. He who vindicates himself does not know God. No one on earth could ever be more authoritative than Christ, yet He never defended Himself. Authority and self-defense are incompatible. The one against whom you defend yourself from may become your judge. He rises higher than you when you begin to answer to his criticism. He who speaks for himself is under judgment. Therefore, he is without authority. Whenever one tries to justify himself, he loses authority." (Nee)

We are to have relationship with the heavenly Father and the Lord Jesus Christ through fellowship and communion, not religiosity and being religious in action or deed. You don't have a relationship with Him because you go to church and do religious things, but because you have fellowship with Him through worship, His Word, and prayer. You are exercising your spirit to hear and know His voice so that you can follow and obey Him and know what He wants you to do.

*"Who gave himself for our sins, that he might deliver us from this present evil world, according to the will of God and our Father"* (Galatians). *"And*

*the Lord shall deliver me from every evil work, and will preserve me unto his heavenly kingdom: to whom be glory forever and ever. Amen."* (2 Timothy 4:18) (Holy Bible King James Version)

Jesus said *"If the Son therefore shall make you free, ye shall be free indeed."* (John 8:36) (Holy Bible King James Version) You will be clean and be of a truth, which is actually freedom. This is an absolute, not a maybe. This is free from all addictions and anything that you don't have control over in your life.

*"For this purpose the Son of God was manifested, that he might destroy the works of the devil."* (1 John 3:8) (Holy Bible King James Version) Bondages can be spiritual, but they can also be physical or emotional. You can be bound by a soul tie created from an ungodly relationship. You can have emotional hurts and scars that come from divorce, death, physical abuse, and mental abuse. Then there is that which comes from demonic activity because of sins against God such as being involved with occult practices or witchcraft in the family. Many are bound by fear, such as a fear of dying, fear of the unknown, fear of living, and a general fear of everything. How can you live victorious in two different and opposite circumstances; in abundance or in lack? Others are bound by unforgiveness. This will stop you from receiving the blessing of God, healing, or deliverance. If you want forgiveness and healing, you have to be willing to forgive.

You can be in bondage to one with a controlling spirit of witchcraft. You can be in bondage to something that is just of your flesh. You can be in bondage and the devil has nothing to do with it. It is just your flesh still being married to the things of the devil and not wanting to stop because your flesh has a mind and will of its own.

When Christ sets us free, it is not freedom to selfishness and seeking our own will, desires, and lusts. It is freedom from them. He sets us free from ourselves and the desires and lusts of the flesh so that we can serve Him and be a blessing to others. We have not been made free to sin, but "free from sin" according to Romans 6:18.

Jesus came to set the captives free, but many in His day were not just in bondage to demons' powers, they were in bondage to man-made religion and doctrines of devils that put them into bondage and took away their spiritual freedom and liberty to serve God in joy and happiness. God never intended for your faith or relationship with Him to put you into bondage and more slavery, but that you might serve him with gladness and joy and rejoicing of spirit. There is none of that in religion and being merely religious. Today many need to be set free from the things they learned and were taught by religion so that they can walk in the freedom and liberty of Christ.

*"Wherein in time past ye walked according to the course of this world, according to the prince of the power of the air, the spirit that now worketh in the children of disobedience: Among whom also we all had our conversation in times past in the lusts of our flesh, fulfilling the desires of the flesh and of the mind; and were by nature the children of wrath, even*

*as others."* (Ephesians 2:2-3) (Holy Bible King James Version) Those who walk in the flesh live to satisfy selfish desires and greed! They live for the satisfaction and pleasure of their flesh. The very nature we were born with was a fallen nature because of sin, and that is why your flesh must be taken to Calvary to die.

All the sinful things that men do are not always help from the devil, but from the lusts of their own flesh because we are sinners by nature. Some people try to put a devil behind every doorknob and around every corner, but they give the devil and his imps far more credit than they deserve, as well as magnify his power and ability beyond that which he has. The devil is NOT omnipresent or omnipotent, only God is. Jesus came to destroy the works of the devil and that includes the works of your fleshly nature so that you would no longer live for the lusts of your flesh.

*"Forasmuch then as Christ hath suffered for us in the flesh, arm yourselves likewise with the same mind: for he that hath suffered in the flesh hath ceased from sin; That he no longer should live the rest of his time in the flesh to the lusts of men, but to the will of God."* (1 Peter 4:1-2) *"But put ye on the Lord Jesus Christ, and make not provision for the flesh, to fulfill the lusts thereof" "This I say then, Walk in the Spirit, and ye shall not fulfill the lust of the flesh. For the flesh lusteth against the Spirit, and the Spirit against the flesh: and these are contrary the one to the other: so that ye cannot do the things that ye would. But if ye be led of the Spirit, ye are not under the law."* (Galatians 5:16-18)

If you're under the law, you're under the law of sin and death. The end result of sin is bondage; bondage to sin and its results. *"If we live in the Spirit, let us also walk in the Spirit."* (Galatians 5:25) This is where there is freedom and liberty in Christ. (Holy Bible King James Version)

When you can die, your flesh walks by the spirit of God, and there is liberty. *"Where the spirit of the Lord is there is liberty."* (**2 Corinthians 3:17**) Verse **18** goes on to say, *"But we all, with open face beholding as in a glass the glory of the Lord, are changed into the same image from glory to glory, even as by the Spirit of the Lord."* Where the spirit is ministering in your life, there is liberty and freedom. The Greek word for freedom is *metamorphoo*. There is a transformation or a metamorphosis taking place in your life, and there is an ever increasing glory. A transformation into glory occurs and to the place of unveiled faces; as Moses was in the presence of God. Moses was without the veil that he used to cover his face because of the glory of God that came upon him. (Holy Bible King James Version)

To know Christ is to know the spirit. To know Christ is to have the spirit. To have the spirit is to have life and freedom; for when the spirit of God comes into your life, He will transform your life and you will not be the same as you were yesterday. This is an ever increasing change as you are taken from glory to glory, being more like Him, and walking and living in His presence, where there is His power, liberty, and freedom.

The Spirit of God comes to fill you that He might transform you and make you like Jesus; the kind of person He was and is. Jesus was never enslaved by the law like the Pharisees, such as their slavery to concepts and ideas of what it meant to keep the Sabbath. This made the law which was spiritual, into physical slavery for the people. When you are filled with and led by the spirit of God, then you can serve God in freedom and in love without bondage to law. Then the glory that is in Christ will continually increase in you and progress in the experience of life and freedom that is given by Christ and by the Spirit now living within you.

    Legalists who would put you into bondage to law and suggest that being freed from the law or not under the Law of Moses means that you would be free from morality or moral character could not be further from the truth. Here Paul is teaching just the opposite. The reality and truth is that morality cannot and does not come by the law, but only by the gift of the spirit of God who lives in freedom from the law for the power of God alone. He lives in the power of faith in God and His word alone can bring a man to righteousness and can produce in your life the fruit of the spirit which cannot come by the keeping of law.

    As you can see, bondage and deliverance is a broad subject. Jesus came to set the captives free, but many in His day were not just in bondage to demons powers, they were in bondage to man-made religion and doctrines. This took away their spiritual freedom and liberty to serve God in joy and happiness. God never intended for your faith to put you into bondage and more slavery, but that you might serve him with gladness and joy and rejoicing of spirit and there is none of that in religion. Today many need to be set free from the things they learned and were taught by religion. They need to realize that they can walk in the freedom and liberty of Christ.

Some of us are in bondage to ideas or things we learned and images in our minds. However, God wants us to be transformed by the renewing of our mind. The children of Israel came out of Egypt, but were still in bondage in their minds. They were still slaves in their thinking and so they did not think or act as free men. Therefore, they were not able to go in and possess the land. God had to wait for a new generation, that wasn't born in slavery and didn't know slavery so that He could give them the Promised Land. *"Blessed be the God and Father of our Lord Jesus Christ, who hath blessed us with all spiritual blessings in heavenly places in Christ:"* (Ephesians 1:3) God wants to give us all the blessings of heaven, but He can't do it if we still think as slaves. We can only receive them by being raised up with Christ and seated with Him in the heavenly where we belong and where our citizenship is. (Comparative Study Bible NIV/Amplified/KJV/Updated NASB)

*"And hath raised us up together, and made us sit together in heavenly places in Christ Jesus: That in the ages to come he might show the exceeding riches of his grace in his kindness toward us through Christ Jesus."* (Ephesians 2:6-7) Have you been seated with Christ to rule, reign in life, and walk in the power and victory of the life of Christ? Have you been freed from all bondages and things

that keep you from the fullness of the liberty and freedom of Christ? (Holy Bible King James Version)

Ruth Graham states "When we fail to follow God's plan for our lives, the Bible calls that behavior sin, and when we sin against God, other people, ourselves, and God, in the form of the Holy Spirit, begins to work in our hearts to cause us to feel remorse for what we have done. (Graham)

## Chapter 12

## Relationship

Relationships are part of the creation design. We were created to need relationships. In order to have healthy relationships with ourselves and others, we must first see ourselves through God's eyes and have a growing relationship with him, our Creator. After all, who could understand us better than the One who wired us? Let's take a look at the first human relationship God created. In Genesis 2:18-23 *"The Lord God said, "It is not good for the man to be alone. I will make him a helper suitable for him."* (Comparative Study Bible NIV/Amplified/KJV/Updated NASB) So, the Lord made a woman from the rib of Adam and brought her to him. Adam enjoyed the greatest relationship possible—a close intimacy with God, whom he had all to himself.

    In "DNA of relationships", the author states that life is relationships and the rest is just details. Webster defines the meaning of relationship as the state or fact of being related; connection by blood or marriage. It's a particular state of affairs among people related to or dealing with one another. (Smalley)

    When God created man, he created him as a three part being- spirit, soul, and body. It's in our soul where He gave us a free will and the capacity to choose. Sometimes you can't always choose your relationships, but you can choose how you will react in those relationships. From the beginning of time, Adam and Eve had a free will, but they chose to disobey God and started the blame game. Oh, how we love to blame someone else!

We are responsible for our own choices and actions. We cannot change other people, but we are responsible for our own behavior. We must remember in any relationship, whether it's marriage, family, church or work, that if there's a conflict, it is never just about the other person. The problem you have is with yourself. All relationships involve choice or will. When we do realize, we will often find things that we need to change, and then we must choose to change them, even when the change is scary.

The external problem is rarely the real problem. In other words, what appears to be the issue or problem is often not the problem, but just the trigger at that moment or instance. Dr. Smalley states that the core problem is our fear. He defines these fears as fear of being alone. Fear is as old as the Garden of Eden.

Without identifying our own core fear and understanding how we tend to react when our fear buttons gets pushed, then our relationships will suffer every time! Therefore, each one of us is involved in a fear dance. We have a choice about how we react when someone pushes our fear button. Our thoughts determine how we are going to feel and react. We must refuse to focus on what the other person has done. We should come to any relationship with realistic expectation and take personal responsibility of our wrong doing.

Instead of trying to knock down the wall of others, we must respect their wall and create a safe environment. By valuing each other then, we can honor the other person. We have to suspend being judgmental of others. We must be trustworthy with others, dedicating ourselves to treating them as the valuable and vulnerable person that they are.

When we take care of our whole selves in a spiritual, emotional, intellectual, and physical sense, we set ourselves up for healthy relationships. We must learn to rest in God. We must learn to listen quietly and ask Him what He's telling us to do. Then, we will be able to identify our emotions, and evaluate whether or not they are true. Most people will only allow God to associate with them in a surface relationship. Just like any relationship, you have to spend time with each other. Each person must invest in the relationship by talking, sharing, and listening. We must learn things about the other person such as their likes and dislikes. Spending quality time together, knowing how the other person feels, and knowing their heart is very important. What make them happy or sad?

What we want today is a revelation to our consciousness of God within us as omnipotent power, so that we can, by a word or a look accomplish that whereunto the word is sent. We want the manifestation to us of the Father in us, so that we can know Him personally. We want to be conscious of God working in us to will and to do, so that we may work out our salvation.

We have been learning how to do the outworking, but have now come to a point where we must learn more of how to place ourselves in an attitude where we can each be conscious of the divine inner working.

## Chapter 13

## Life Healing Changes

Life Healing Changes are based on the idea that the Bible is God's chosen tool to equip believers for every event in life, (2 Timothy 3:16-17) the final authority of truth, (Psalm 119:160) and the means by which He sanctifies us. (John 17:17) The Word is sufficient enough to enable change in all areas it addresses. (1 Peter 2:1-3) God is faithful to cause the Word to be living and active; reaching a depth of the soul not accessible by man. These are the thoughts and intentions of the heart. (Hebrews 4:12-13) (Holy Bible King James Version)

"*His divine power has given us everything we need for life and godliness through our knowledge of him who called us by his own glory and goodness.*" (2 Peter 1:3) You are to substitute biblical truth for error as you go about your day-to-day lives. They know that the truth, when known, believed, and obeyed, sets people free. When people are set free, they are fulfilling their true calling. "*Then you will know the truth, and the truth will set you free.*" (John 8:32) (Holy Bible King James Version)

Jesus weighed in on the issue when He made the remarkable statement in His marvelous prayer concerning the Bible. "*Sanctify them in the truth; Thy word is truth.*" (John 17:17) Wow! That is powerful stuff! Since the Bible is truth given by God, it touches directly and intimately on our lives. (Holy Bible King James Version)

You have lived under the false judgments of others and self for so long that you have come to believe that's who you are. When you accept false judgment, you can lose your destiny. Everyone lives out of self-perception. This is why the Body of Christ is under "identity theft". You must know yourselves according to God.

However, in Proverbs it states a man is still what he thinks in his heart. God's view is usually radically different than our own view of our self. We need to learn how to look within our hearts and discover our true self. Remember Satan attacked Jesus' identity in Matthew 4:3 when he stated that *"If thou be the son of God, command that these stones be made bread"*. Jesus knew the source of His identity; Matthew 4:4. But he answered and said, *"It is written"*. Satan wanted Jesus to prove who He was by works, but Jesus knew that what God had spoken was all the proof that He needed. (Holy Bible King James Version)

*"For the word of God is living and active. Sharper than any double-edged sword, it penetrates even to dividing soul and spirit, joints and marrow; it judges the thoughts and attitudes of the heart"* (Hebrews 4:12). So, therefore what God has spoken to you is all the proof that you need. (Comparative Study Bible NIV/Amplified/KJV/ Updated NASB)

After all, Paul says, *"All Scripture is inspired by God and profitable for teaching, for reproof, for correction, for training in righteousness"* (2 Timothy 3:16). He also wrote, *"Be diligent to present yourself approved to God as a workman who does not need to be ashamed, handling accurately the word of truth."*

(2 Timothy 2:15 Comparative Study Bible NIV/Amplified/KJV/ Updated NASB)

When you discover the real you, the pathway to your destiny will be clear. Your destiny waits for you - the real you in Christ. But most people are afraid of what they will find within their own hearts. We are new on the inside so therefore, we must put on the renewed mind because without it, we will see our old self before we were saved. It's imperative that we get our thinking straight on who we truly are. Ephesians 4:24 says *"and ye put on the new man, which after God is created in righteousness and true holiness"*. (Holy Bible King James Version)

Accepting God's judgment removes us from our own limitations. You can live a life carved out of your personal history or you can live a life shaped and controlled by the truth that God has given you. When your perception becomes God's perception, then you can surely do all things through Christ. But, if you do not believe that you deserve success then every cell in your body will work toward that end.

Spend every day establishing your mind into your new identity and your life and body will follow your mind and its beliefs. Believe God and prosper; believe your old man and you will live only what your flesh can produce. When you believe I am worth what God paid for me, the greater the need we have for self-worth and the more sensitive we are to the actions of others. Low self-worth thrives on judgment like a drug addict thrives on drugs. Our sense of value largely is determined by how we see ourselves in Christ or by how we see ourselves in relation to others.

You must deal with self before you attempt to deal with others. Matthew 7:3-5 *"Why do you look at the speck in your brother's eye, but do not notice the log in your own eye? Or how can you say to your brother, Let me take the speck out of your eye, and look there's a log in your eye? Hypocrite! First take the log out of your own eye, and then you will see clearly to take the speck out of your brother's eye".* (Holman Illustrated Study Bible)

When you seek to fix someone else, you have rejected them. Being right does not qualify you to correct others. Being right creates battles between other people who also believe they are right. Trying to fix others implies superiority and control. Your log in your eye will blind you to the true needs of another person. Then you can become more focused on proving your judgment than being open to the truth.

You are free to live in peace and love. Accept all that Jesus paid for you now. Life is too short to live any other way. Biblical healing is the bedrock of life. The Bible tells us about who we are, why we are here, why we exist, how to live life, and where we go after this life. It tells us who God is, how He relates to and treats His creation, and what He expects. In short, the Bible gives us hope, certainty, direction, instruction, inspiration, and a sense of meaning and purpose to life – both this life and the next one yet to come.

2 Peter 1:3 states *"seeing that His divine power hath granted to us everything pertain to life and godliness, through the true knowledge of Him who called us by His own glory and excellence".*

(Comparative Study Bible NIV/Amplified/KJV/ Updated NASB) God has all the answers to life but according to the knowledge of Him. Healing is mastering and living a successful life while the world around us swirls with a gaggle of voices and opinions like a dust storm in Arizona, or a hurricane in Florida.

## Chapter 14

### Conquering your Flesh

The power of God is in His Word. When that logo becomes Rhema in our spirit, then the Spirit of God uses it to make a change and transformation in us.

We think *Look I'm saved, I'm born again, I have the spirit of God in me. Why do I keep sinning and doing the wrong thing? I just can't seem to overcome my flesh.* You can overcome the flesh and live in God's abundance by walking in the spirit and not fulfilling the lusts of the flesh. How do you do that? We need to find out how to be led by the spirit and stop walking in the flesh and how to walk in life and victory.

The flesh is a way of thinking that leads to bad decisions that leads to failure. Failure doesn't come from being in the flesh or being out of control in your emotions; failure comes from making bad decisions and bad decisions come from being in the flesh and from letting your emotions rule over you.

The enemy of our inheritance is not the devil, but the flesh. The devil doesn't stop us from walking in the spirit and having what God wants us to have but our flesh does. The flesh opposes the spirit and the spirit opposes the flesh. If you are not walking in your inheritance, it is because you are not walking in the spirit, but in the flesh.

"*It is the spirit that quickeneth; the flesh profiteth nothing: the words that I speak unto you, they are spirit, and they are life*" (John 6:63). (Holy Bible King James Version) The spirit quickens and it gives life. The flesh profits nothing. If the flesh profits nothing, then there is no benefit in doing it. Why do people walk in the flesh? It isn't because they have to, but because they choose to, especially if they have been redeemed. Most people walk in the flesh because they think it will accomplish something or produce something. Why do people get angry? They think it will cause others to do what they want. They think it will get others to change their behavior or whatever, but the flesh profits nothing. The spirit is the Word of God. To walk in the spirit is to walk in the Word of God. When you walk in the Word, you walk in the spirit for the Word is spirit and life. And if you walk in the Word, you will not walk in the flesh and think and do that which will lead to failure, sin and that which is bad for you.

We are talking about a mindset. What your mind is set on and the basis for your thought life. We are also talking about a worldview. Do you think and see things in this world, in your life and circumstances through the filter of the Word of God? Or is it by what man says, by humanistic thinking, by modern psychology, by that which is convenient to you or that which you think will benefit you? Today's society is being taught to think contrary to the Word of God, to think that they are not a creation of a loving God, to think that God shouldn't be in our society because everyone doesn't believe in God and that there are no moral or other absolutes.

That way of thinking leads people to walk in the flesh, produces the lusts of the flesh and leads us to do that which is contrary to God. So, let us look further at man.

Our spirit is that part of our being that is conscious of what is above us. It was created to be God's conscious. Our soul is that part of our being that is conscious of that which is around us. Our flesh is that part of our being that is conscious of what is wrong with us, and what is in us. Our flesh is that part of our being that is what is in us, not what God has put in us, but what our emotions and that which we feel, see and hear perceives or that which is on us.

There is a part of us that can be conscious of what is above us. What is above us - heaven, God and life says, *"If ye then be risen with Christ, seek those things which are above, where Christ sitteth on the right hand of God. Set your affection on things above, not on things on the earth"* (Colossians 3:1-2). It is where Jesus is *"Far above all principality, and power, and might, and dominion, and every name that is named, not only in this world, but also in that which is to come"* (Ephesians 1:21) and *"Every good gift and every perfect gift is from above, and cometh down from the Father of lights, with whom is no variableness, neither shadow of turning"* (James 1:17). (Comparative Study Bible NIV/Amplified/KJV/ Updated NASB)

*"This I say then, Walk in the Spirit, and ye shall not fulfill the lust of the flesh. For the flesh lusteth against the Spirit, and the Spirit against the flesh: and these are contrary the one to the other: so that ye cannot do the things that ye would"* (Galatians 5:16-17). (Comparative Study Bible NIV/Amplified/KJV/ Updated NASB) The flesh is at war against the spirit and the spirit is at war against

the flesh. They are fighting one another and you can't do the things you want or desire and you can't have what you want. The war between the flesh and spirit will keep you from having the things you wish, desire or that God wants you to have. So we have to put an end to the flesh.

The Bible doesn't say battle your flesh, but crucify your flesh *"But put ye on the Lord Jesus Christ, and make not provision for the flesh, to fulfill the lusts thereof"* (Romans 13:14). *"And they that are Christ's have crucified the flesh with the affections and lusts. If we live in the Spirit, let us also walk in the Spirit"* (Galatians 5:24-25). That means to walk in the power and by the leading of the Holy Spirit. *"And thine ears shall hear a word behind thee, saying, This is the way, walk ye in it, when ye turn to the right hand, and when ye turn to the left"* (Isaiah 30:21). (Comparative Study Bible NIV/Amplified/KJV/ Updated NASB) What is that word you will hear? that spirit speaking to you God's Word, bringing a verse to mind, causing your consciousness to be pricked because of the truth you know, what God has commanded you to do and how He has told us to live?

Look at this verse, *"And I will bring the blind by a way that they knew not; I will lead them in paths that they have not known: I will make darkness light before them, and crooked things straight. These things will I do unto them, and not forsake them"* (Isaiah 42:16). (Comparative Study Bible NIV/Amplified/KJV/ Updated NASB) How does God do this? To bring one from darkness to light is by the revelation of God's Word. Christ told Paul that he was sending him to preach the gospel to *"To open their eyes, and to turn them from darkness to light, and from the power of Satan unto God* puts it this way, *"We have also a more sure word of prophecy; whereunto ye do well that ye take heed, as unto a light that shineth in a dark place, until the day dawn, and the day star arise in your hearts"* (Acts 26:18; 2 Peter 1:19). That is because God's word is the light. *"The entrance of thy words giveth light"* (Psalm 119:130). The Word of God brings light into the mind. That which is contrary to the word of God is darkness and blindness of the mind. 2 Corinthians 4:4 brings these two things together. *"In whom the god of this world hath blinded the minds of them which believe not, lest the light of the glorious gospel of Christ, who is the image of God, should shine unto them."* (Comparative Study Bible NIV/Amplified/KJV/ Updated NASB)

That thinking which is contrary to truth is thinking which is not according to truth or that which is a lie. Romans 3:4 says *"let God be true, but every man a liar."* (Comparative Study Bible NIV/Amplified/KJV/ Updated NASB) Any thought that is contrary to truth is a lie. The truth of God's Word is light. So any thinking that is contrary to the light of God's Word is darkness. God's Word is spirit and life and all thinking that is contrary to God's Word is flesh and death.

*"There is therefore now no condemnation to them which are in Christ Jesus, who walk not after the flesh, but after the Spirit"* (Romans 8:1). (Holy Bible King James Version) To walk after the Spirit is to walk under the authority and under the obedience

of the Word. If you walk contrary to the Word you are walking according to the fleshly mind and that brings condemnation because you are in disobedience to the Word. Therefore, it continues, *"For the law of the Spirit of life in Christ Jesus hath made me free from the law of sin and death"* (Romans 8:2). (Holy Bible King James Version) When you walk in the fleshly mind, you will make wrong decisions that lead to sin and sin leads to death.

    Scripture says that you have to take up your cross daily, not fight your flesh daily and that is because the flesh tries to resurrect itself. *"If any man will come after me, let him deny himself, and take up his cross daily, and follow me"* (Luke 9:23). (Holy Bible King James Version) What is your cross? Your cross is where your will, your desire, your thoughts are contrary to the thoughts, will and desire of God for your life. It is where your will and the will of God come into conflict and you have to do as Jesus when He walked as a man and pray, "Father… not my will, but thine, be done" (Luke 22:42). Why is this true? We can verify this with another scripture. *"For my thoughts are not your thoughts, neither are your ways my ways, saith the LORD. For as the heavens are higher than the earth, so are my ways higher than your ways, and my thoughts than your thoughts"* (Isaiah 55:8-9). (Holy Bible King James Version) So when we are following our ways, our thoughts, that is walking in the flesh because it is contrary to God's ways and God's thoughts which are given to us through His Word.

But you have to crucify your flesh once and for all. That is done by your coming to the cross and surrendering your life and identifying with His death, burial and resurrection, which is shown in baptism. Therein through baptism we tell the world that we have died to our self and living by our flesh, the ways that are contrary to God's Word and now are a new creation in Christ Jesus and will walk according to His Word and His Spirit. You crucify your flesh by identifying the flesh to the simplest definition and then you won't have to constantly battle it.

You won't have to think, now does my flesh want to eat a piece of pie or whatever. At the simplest definition, the flesh is the opposite of the spirit. *"Verily, verily, I say unto you, Except ye eat the flesh of the Son of man, and drink his blood, ye have no life in you. Whoso eateth my flesh, and drinketh my blood, hath eternal life; and I will raise him up at the last day. For my flesh is meat indeed, and my blood is drink indeed. He that eateth my flesh, and drinketh my blood, dwelleth in me, and I in him. As the living Father hath sent me, and I live by the Father: so he that eateth me, even he shall live by me. This is that bread which came down from heaven: not as your fathers did eat manna, and are dead: he that eateth of this bread shall live forever"* (John 6:53-58). (Holy Bible King James Version)

So what is Jesus talking about here? This passage is twofold. In this passage there is an indirect application in the Lord Supper, but in this context it is primarily speaking about His Word. Yes, we remember His life and death by partaking of the elements of Lord Supper and thereby identify with His sacrifice for us and come back to the cross and apply it to our lives.

But more importantly, Jesus was the Word become flesh, the Living Bread that came down from heaven and we live by Him by eating His Word and living by His Word, which is our heavenly manna. Jesus lived by the Father by living by His Word and so do we. *"I can of mine own self do nothing: as I hear, I judge"* (John 5:30). (Holy Bible King James Version)

Concerning the Body of Christ, Jesus said *"Verily, verily, I say unto you, He that heareth my word, and believeth on him that sent me, hath everlasting life, and shall not come into condemnation; but is passed from death unto life"* (John 5:24) (Holy Bible King James Version). How do you pass from death and condemnation into life? By hearing the Word and believing His Word which means to live by His Word and allow it to influence and control our decisions. *"If ye continue in my word, then are ye my disciples indeed; And ye shall know the truth, and the truth shall make you free."* (John 8:31-32). (Holy Bible King James Version) The truth is God's Word is what sets us free from all lies and deceptions of the world and the devil and walking by His Word is what makes us His disciples. Walking in the flesh is walking contrary to God's Word.

The Words of Jesus are the Spirit of God, walking in the spirit is walking in the Word. Walking in the flesh is walking contrary to the Word and it happens without thought because it is a mindset and that is why our minds must be renewed by the Word of God. *"And be not conformed to this world:* (don't be made in the image of this world, to look and act like the world, we are to be conformed to the image of Christ) *but be ye transformed* (totally changed in nature so as to make fit for a totally new purpose so that your outward man looks like the inward spirit of Christ) *by the renewing of your mind* (by the living and abiding Word of God within)*, that ye may prove what is that good, and acceptable, and perfect, will of God"* (Romans 12:2). The only way to transform your mind and thinking is by filling it with the Word of God and walking according to the Word of God is the only way to prove that good and acceptable and perfect will of God for your life. (Holy Bible King James Version)

    I sinned, I fell, and I blew it. Does that mean I was in the flesh? No. It's being in the flesh that caused you to sin, to blow it. Being in the flesh is not an action, but a way of thinking. It is a disease condition of the soul that leads to corrupt decisions and that is where failure comes from. The flesh is a way of thinking that leads to a decision against God's Word that leads to bad decisions to being out of control in your emotions. Bad decisions come from being emotionally ruled instead of ruling over them, it is a way of thinking that opposed the Word and opposes righteousness. The flesh stays alive through a system of thoughts.

    Therefore the flesh is crucified by taking thoughts captive. *"Casting down imaginations, and every high thing that exalteth itself against the knowledge of God, and bringing into captivity every thought to the obedience of Christ"* (2 Corinthians 10:5 Holy Bible King James Version) Imaginations speaks of images in the mind and those images that come from worldly, carnal, ungodly thinking must be cast down because they are contrary to Christ. God said bring your thoughts into line with my Word, into obedience of His Word and that is what it is to bring them into the obedience of Christ. You can only do that by displacing incorrect thinking with the Word of God, by filling your mind with God's Word that you will then walk and make decisions according to that Word.

    That is what the word to Joshua was all about in Joshua 1:8. *"This book of the law shall not depart out of thy mouth; but thou shalt meditate therein day and night, that thou mayest observe to do according to all that is written therein: for then thou shalt make thy way prosperous, and then thou shalt have good success."* (Holy Bible King James Version) When you fill your mind with His Word, you meditate on His Word and it is in your heart, then you will speak it and do according to it and then you will have success because you will be walking according to the spirit and not the flesh.

    The Bible states *"That the righteousness of the law might be fulfilled in us, who walk not after the flesh, but after the Spirit"* (Romans 8:4). (Holy Bible King James Version) Righteousness is fulfilled by the spirit, by walking in the spirit. Those in the flesh mind the things of the flesh and those in the spirit have their minds on the things of the Word. *"For they that are after the flesh do mind the things of the flesh; but they that are after the Spirit the things of the Spirit. For to be carnally* (worldly) *minded is death; but to be spiritually* (Word) *minded is life and peace"* (Romans 8:5-6). To be fleshly minded, carnally minded is death. The flesh is a way of thought, a way of thinking, of words that are contrary to the scripture and to Jesus. It is not that the flesh wants this or that. It is a way of thinking that leads to immorality; that leads to lust and other works of the flesh. The words of the flesh lead to the works of the flesh in Galatians 5:19-21. Lasciviousness is living without boundaries. This list of the works of the flesh, are the manifestations of a wrong way of thinking. The flesh is simply a wrong way of thinking, a wrong attitude of the mind, a wrong mindset.

    The flesh is not thinking of lusting things. No the flesh produces lustful things. Lustful things are the fruit, the harvest of the flesh. The flesh is not thinking "that sin that I did, that will finish me off; that will doom me." You wouldn't think that that thought is the flesh talking to you, but that is what it is; because it is contrary to what the Word says. No sin or failure has to result in your ultimate doom. The word says God will remove our sins as far as the east is from the west when we repent of them. The Word says, *"If we confess our sins, he is faithful and just to forgive us our sins, and to cleanse us from all unrighteousness"* (1 John 1:9). (Holy Bible King James Version) God is faithful and just to forgive. Our part is to humble ourselves and repent of that sin and then change our way of thinking, that is the about face of repentance, so that we do not go back to that sin and continually walk in that sin we have repented of. It is done by a change of mind, a change of thinking. Repentance is first and foremost a change in attitude of the mind and therefore a change in direction.

When we think, "I don't know if I will ever get over this sickness." That is the flesh, not the spirit because it is not the Word of God. There is a diffcrence between the manifestation of the flesh, the byproducts of the flesh and what it is. The sprit says, "I can do all things through Christ which strengthens me," and the flesh says, "If I just do this or that, I can do it myself."

The flesh's appetite is fed by a wrong thought pattern that leads to fleshly actions and sin. "I don't know if I can do this, if I can stop doing this, or get victory over that." That is the flesh. The flesh opposes the sprit, which is the Word that says "I can do all things through Christ who strengthens me." It is not I can do all things. That is also fleshly thinking that will bring us into condemnation before God because it is pride in our ability rather than faith in His ability to work in us and enable us to do it and pride comes before destruction.

We cannot do what He asks in and of ourselves or by our flesh. We can only obey and do God's will by the empowerment of the Holy Spirit dwelling within us. Yes, the Spirit of God can work and lead a new believer in that which is right, even though he or she doesn't yet know the Word concerning something, but still can convict of God's desire for us and lead us in the right way. Yes, but the problem is our thinking being by a worldly, humanistic mindset that has to be changed by the washing of the water of the Word, which bring sanctification, which is a process and doesn't happen all at once. It is when we see ourselves in the mirror of the Word and see that we are doing something that God doesn't want or not doing what He does, that we change our thinking in that area and ask the Lord to enable us to then do that which is right, but it begins with your changing your thinking so that it is according to His Word. Why, because scripture tells us this about man, *"For as he thinketh in his heart, so is he"* (Proverbs 23:7). (Comparative Study Bible NIV/Amplified/KJV/ Updated NASB) That is because you first think, then you do or act on what you think or meditate upon. You become according to your thinking. So you're thinking and your life are either being conformed to the image of Christ by being conformed to His Word or you are being conformed to the image of Lucifer by your thinking more and more like the world and its ways.

*"Let no man say when he is tempted, I am tempted of God: for God cannot be tempted with evil, neither tempteth he any man: But every man is tempted, when he is drawn away of his own lust, and enticed. Then when lust hath conceived, it bringeth forth sin: and sin, when it is finished, bringeth forth death"* (James 1:13-15). (Comparative Study Bible NIV/Amplified/KJV/ Updated NASB) How are you tempted? In your mind! It is by thoughts of the mind that temptation comes. Then the question is what you do when a bad or evil thought comes. It isn't the first look or first sight that is or causes lust and adultery in the mind, but the second look that continues to look and admire and think upon. No one ever robbed

a bank or another person without thought and planning. It begins in the mind. No one lied without thought to try and conceal truth to protect themselves or whatever. What you think upon, you will move toward and then you will do it and sin and if you continue in it that continual sin will lead to spiritual death. It is that simple. You once made a decision for Christ, okay, but that isn't good enough. It isn't where you begin the race but where you finish it. You must continually choose to follow Jesus. You still have a free will. Many have and when they walk in the flesh and according to its lusts; that leads to spiritual death as with the prodigal son. But yet, God in His great mercy; allows for repentance and restoration of the prodigal who turned away from His grace. That is grace beyond understanding and love I cannot comprehend.

Again, the flesh says I'm afraid, I can't believe that, that isn't going to work. That is the flesh. Your right, the flesh doesn't believe anything but self. It only believes what it can see, touch, hear and smell. The flesh lives by its five senses and the flesh can't please God. *"Because the carnal mind is enmity against God: for it is not subject to the law of God, neither indeed can be. So then they that are in the flesh cannot please God"* (Romans 8:7-8). (Holy Bible King James Version) The carnal, fleshly mind is hatred against God and the things of God and it cannot be subject to the Word of God. Why can't you please God in the flesh? Because the flesh lives by what you see and if you live by what you see you can't live by faith and without faith it is impossible to please God. The Bible states "F*aith cometh by* *hearing, and hearing by the word of God*" (Romans 10:17). *"But without faith it is impossible to please him: for he that cometh to God must believe that he is, and that he is a rewarder of them that diligently seek him"* (Hebrews 11:6). (Holy Bible King James Version) The opposite of faith is the flesh. Faith comes from hearing the word. Fear comes from hearing your flesh, something contrary to the word of God.

How do you think righteousness? Righteousness becomes the filter of your mind. Nothing can go through your mind without asking righteousness decision. Every thought that comes into your head needs to stop at the registration desk and check in with righteousness and let righteousness decide whether to allow that thought in or not. We must come to victory and become what God wants us to be, conformed to the image of Christ. *"For whom he did foreknow, he also did predestinate to be conformed to the image of his Son."* (Romans 8:19 Comparative Study Bible NIV /Amplified/KJV/ Updated NASB) The registration of your mind must be righteousness, God's righteousness.

Remember your thought life controls your actions and the flesh is a way of thinking. If you think the way God tells you to think, then you will see results and you will get victory over your flesh and its desires. The key is to take charge over your flesh by taking charge over the fleshly thought life and mindset and bring it into the obedience of Christ. This is the key to walking in the spirit.

Walking in the spirit first takes filling your mind with the Word of God and then prayer and learning to become sensitive to the Spirit of God by practice and exercising your spirit and faith in everyday life. *"But ye are not in the flesh, but in the Spirit, if so be that the Spirit of God dwell in you. Now if any man have not the Spirit of Christ, he is none of his. And if Christ be in you, the body is dead because of sin; but the Spirit is life because of righteousness."* (Romans 8: 9-10) (Holy Bible King James Version)

We have to remember, that it must always begin with being born again of the spirit of God. The natural man, not born of the Spirit, cannot walk according to the Spirit of God, cannot be led by the Spirit of God, cannot have his mind renewed by the Spirit of God, which uses the Word of God to renew and cleanse the mind of the things of the world and the past life, when we come to Christ and walk with Him. But if you have come to Christ, you have come to the cross and put your faith in the finished works of Calvary and the blood of Jesus shed for your sin, then the Spirit of God comes into your life and that will bring life and righteousness. *"But of him are ye in Christ Jesus, who of God is made unto us wisdom, and righteousness, and sanctification, and redemption"* (1 Corinthians 1:20). (Holy Bible King James Version)

The Spirit must first convict the sinner using the Word of God to bring them to repentance and then He can do His work of salvation and renewing of the spirit within man that makes us born-again. "But according to his mercy he saved us, by the washing of regeneration, and renewing of the Holy Ghost.;" (Titus 3:5). (Comparative Study Bible NIV/Amplified/KJV/ Updated NASB)

We must begin with the Spirit by being born of the Spirit and then we must continue in the Spirit, allowing Him to renew our minds by His Word as we read and study and meditate upon it and then allowing Him to speak to us in our daily life and become sensitive to His leading that we know His voice and leading and then we will find a new level of success and victory in life and we think according to His Word and allow it to direct our decisions in life.

*"But be ye doers of the word, and not hearers only, deceiving your own selves. For if any be a hearer of the word, and not a doer, he is like unto a man beholding his natural face in a glass: For he beholdeth himself, and goeth his way, and straightway forgetteth what manner of man he was. But whoso looketh into the perfect law of liberty, and continueth therein, he being not a forgetful hearer, but a doer of the work, this man shall be blessed in his deed"* (James 1:15-22). (Holy Bible King James Version) It does no good to read or hear the Word if it goes in one ear and out the other and we do not hear, believe and then act according. When God's Word shows us the way and rebukes something in our life, then we need to allow it to cleanse our lifestyle by cleansing and renewing our thinking. Then we will walk according to His Word and Spirit and be doers of the Word and receive the blessing of God. The one, who hears only, doesn't receive the blessing and the inheritance, but the one who is a

doer because He allows His thinking to be changed and conformed to the Word of God, which conform us to the image of Christ.

*"Therefore, brethren, we are debtors, not to the flesh, to live after the flesh. For if ye live after the flesh, ye shall die: but if ye through the Spirit do mortify the deeds of the body, ye shall live. For as many as are led by the Spirit of God, they are the sons of God.* You must walk as a son of God to be a son of God. To be a son is to come under the authority of your spiritual Father. To be a part of His kingdom, you have to be under the authority of the King. That is what sonship is about, not just confessing, "I am a son of God." (Romans 8:12-14). (Holy Bible King James Version)

You are what you do, not what you claim by profession. If the Word is directing your life and decision, therefore your actions, then you are being led by the Spirit of God, for His Word is spirit and life. *"It is the spirit that quickeneth; the flesh profiteth nothing: the words that I speak unto you, they are spirit, and they are life. But there are some of you that believe not"* (John 6:63-64). (Holy Bible King James Version)

# Bibliography

Allen, David Dr. In Search of the Heart. Nashville: Thomas Nelson Publishers, 1993.
Bullock, Ada Dr. "Forgetting those things which are behind." Oiver Branch, 3 February 2009.
Bynum, Juanita Ph. D. Matters of the Heart. Lake Mary: Charisma House, 2002.
Cady, H. Emilie. Lessons in Truth. Kansas: Unity School of Christianity, 1961.
Comparative Study Bible NIV/Amplified/KJV/ Updated NASB. Grand Rapids: Zondervan, 1999.
www.faithdome.org,11 April 2010 Faith to Walk in the Spirit. By Betty Dr Price and Fredrick Dr. Price.
Graham, Ruth. Broken Heart. Grand Rapids: Zondervan, 2004.
Hebrew-Greek. Hebrew-Greek Key Word Study Bible / King James. Chattanooga: AMG, Revised 1991.
Holman Illustrated Study Bible. Nashville: Holman Bible Publishers, 2006.
Holy Bible King James Version. Nashville: Thomas Nelson Publishers, 1994.
http://christianity.helium.com/topic/4033-bible-study. 25 April 2010.
Moore, Beth. Breaking Free: NashvilleBroadman & Holman Publishers
Nee, Watchman. The Spiritual Man. Richmond: Christian Fellowship Publishers, Inc, 1977.
Nelson's Illustrated Bible Dictionary. Chattanooga: Thomas Nelson, 1986.
Richardson, Gary L. Fear is Never Your Friend. Tulsa: HonorNet, 2006.
Self, Ray Dr. "Essential Christian Doctrines." Oliver Branch: International College of Ministry, 23 July 2009.

Shaw, C Elizabeth. "Renewing the Mind / International College of Ministry." Olive Branch, 23 January 2010.

Smalley, Gray Dr. the DNA of Relationships. Colorado Springs: Smalley Publishung Group LLC, 2007.

The Master's Healing Presence Bible King James Version. United States: Thomas Nelson Bibles / A Divison of Thomas Nelson, Inc., 2003.

Webster's II. Boston: Houghton Mifflin Company, 2001.

## ABOUT THE AUTHOR

Dr. Glenda Akiens is an Apostle to the nations; she and her husband serve as apostolic Covering for ministries all over the world. As she flows in the office of Prophet, teaching and preaching the uncompromising Word of God with miracles, signs and wonders following, God arrested her attention and illuminated His Words – "to whom much is given much is required" and "before I formed thee in the belly I knew thee; before I brought you forth out of the womb I ordained you a prophet unto the nations." Dr. Akiens is truly one of America's modern day prophetic voices.

Dr. Akiens and her husband Apostle Latera Akiens are Pastors of Restoration International Ministries and New Beginning Kingdom Ministries, in Waco Texas. She is founder of Restoration Apostolic Prayer Line, she serve as a Chaplain in Germantown, TN, formerly International Intercessors for Full Gospel. Dr. Akiens is mentoring parent and counselor to other ministries. She is the CEO of "Let's Talk Real Talk Girl Talk and "Let's Talk Real Talk", CEO of Restoration Counseling, and she serves as a Director of International College of Ministry in Orlando, FL.. She is also CEO of Joshua Emmanuel Foundation.

Dr. Akiens is a graduate of International College of Ministry. During her studies, she acquired a Ph.D. in Philosophy in Christian Psychology. These accomplishments were acquired through the International College of Ministry as well as the Wisdom of God International College, Calvary Bible

Institute, and Sarasota Academy of Christian Counseling.

Her ministry has carried her into the areas of prison ministry, homeless ministry, counseling, and deliverance ministry. Pulling on her background in corporate, government, human resources, and psychology, Dr. Akiens translates hard-hitting spiritual insights into everyday language that empowers individuals to transform their lives, helping them to walk in their divine purpose and walk out their destiny.

As the anointed mother of six children and five grandchildren, she possesses an uncanny ability to reach people of all ages and from various walks of life. Through her ministry, she strives to positively influence the lives of God's people through the application of the Word of Truth. She continues to immensely impact thousands of lives as she flows in the divinely appointed office of apostle, effectively ministering the total ministry of the Kingdom of God. Her endeavor is to empower the Body of Christ to reach and experience their God-given rights as sons and daughters of the Most High God. She is under the mantle of Elijah!

**CONTACT INFORMATION**
Dr. Glenda Akiens
Restoration International Ministry
P.O. Box 152
Collierville, TN 38027
(404) 919-3182

Made in the USA
San Bernardino, CA
17 April 2015